roofing

step by step

CREATIVE HOMEOWNER®, Upper Saddle River, New Jersey

SMART GUIDE: ROOFING

MANAGING EDITOR	Fran Donegan
PROOFREADER	Sara Markowitz
PHOTO COORDINATOR	Mary Dolan
INDEXER	Schroeder Indexing Services
DIGITAL IMAGING SPECIALIST	Frank Dyer
SMART GUIDE® SERIES COVER DESIGN	Clarke Barre
FRONT COVER PHOTOGRAPHY	John Puleio/CH

CREATIVE HOMEOWNER

VICE PRESIDENT AND PUBLISHER	Timothy O. Bakke
MANAGING EDITOR	Fran J. Donegan
ART DIRECTOR	David Geer
PRODUCTION COORDINATOR	Sara M. Markowitz

Current Printing (last digit)
10 9 8 7 6 5 4 3 2 1

Manufactured in the United States of America

Smart Guide: Roofing, Second Edition
Library of Congress Control Number: 2009933310
ISBN-10: 1-58011-480-6
ISBN-13: 978-1-58011-480-6

CREATIVE HOMEOWNER®
A Division of Federal Marketing Corp.
24 Park Way
Upper Saddle River, NJ 07458
www.creativehomeowner.com

contents

safety first

Though all the designs and methods in this book have been reviewed for safety, it is not possible to overstate the importance of using safe construction methods. What follows are reminders; some do's and don'ts of basic carpentry. They are not substitutes for your own common sense.

- *Always* use caution, care, and good judgment when following the procedures described in this book.

- *Always* be sure that the electrical setup is safe; be sure that no circuit is overloaded and that all power tools and electrical outlets are properly grounded. Do not use power tools in wet locations.

- *Always* read container labels on paints, solvents, and other products; provide ventilation, and observe all other warnings.

- *Always* read the manufacturer's instructions for using a tool, especially the warnings.

- *Always* use hold-downs and push sticks whenever possible when working on a table saw. Avoid working short pieces if you can.

- *Always* remove the key from any drill chuck (portable or press) before starting the drill.

- *Always* pay deliberate attention to how a tool works so that you can avoid being injured.

- *Always* know the limitations of your tools. Do not try to force them to do what they were not designed to do.

- *Always* make sure that any adjustment is locked before proceeding. For example, always check the rip fence on a table saw or the bevel adjustment on a portable saw before starting to work.

- *Always* clamp small pieces firmly to a bench or other work surface when using a power tool on them.

- *Always* wear the appropriate rubber or work gloves when handling chemicals, moving or stacking lumber, or doing heavy construction.

- *Always* wear a disposable face mask when you create dust by sawing or sanding. Use a special filtering respirator when working with toxic substances and solvents.

- *Always* wear eye protection, especially when using power tools or striking metal on metal or concrete; a chip can fly off, for example, when chiseling concrete.

- *Always* be aware that there is seldom enough time for your body's reflexes to save you from injury from a power tool in a dangerous situation; everything happens too fast. Be *alert!*

- *Always* keep your hands away from the business ends of blades, cutters, and bits.

- *Always* hold a circular saw firmly, usually with both hands so that you know where they are.

- *Always* use a drill with an auxiliary handle to control the torque when large-size bits are used.

- *Always* check your local building codes when planning new construction. The codes are intended to protect public safety and should be observed to the letter.

- *Never* work with power tools when you are tired or under the influence of alcohol or drugs.

- *Never* cut tiny pieces of wood or pipe using a power saw. Cut small pieces off larger pieces.

- *Never* change a saw blade or a drill or router bit unless the power cord is unplugged. Do not depend on the switch being off; you might accidentally hit it.

- *Never* work in insufficient lighting.

- *Never* work while wearing loose clothing, hanging hair, open cuffs, or jewelry.

- *Never* work with dull tools. Have them sharpened, or learn how to sharpen them yourself.

- *Never* use a power tool on a workpiece—large or small—that is not firmly supported.

- *Never* saw a workpiece that spans a large distance between horses without close support on each side of the cut; the piece can bend, closing on and jamming the blade, causing saw kickback.

- *Never* support a workpiece from underneath with your leg or other part of your body when sawing.

- *Never* carry sharp or pointed tools, such as utility knives, awls, or chisels, in your pocket. If you want to carry such tools, use a special-purpose tool belt with leather pockets and holders.

introduction

Roofs demand our attention. On many homes, the roof is visible from the street and contributes to the curb appeal of the building, so it is important to pick a roofing product that enhances the design of the house. And a roof that leaks often leads to big problems, including damage to the homeowner's belongings and the structure itself.

Smart Guide: Roofing provides a quick reference to help you select the right roofing product, whether you are applying a new roof or reroofing over an existing roof. You will find information on all of the major roofing materials, including asphalt shingles, wood shakes and shingles, tile, slate, metal, and the new composite materials. This book will show you how to prepare an existing roof for new material, weatherproof joints with flashing, estimate materials, install roofing, and work safely.

And because a long-lasting roof requires adequate roof and attic ventilation to function properly, there is a chapter to help you select the type of ventilation system and the amount of vent area that are best for your house. A final chapter covers roof repairs, including replacing shingles and patching flashing—valuable information to help you find and stop leaks fast.

chapter 1

roofing basics

Roofing Language

Standing out in the yard with a pair of binoculars at the ready, you might be mistaken for a bird watcher by your neighbors. How would they know you are only following the advice of the Asphalt Roofing Manufacturers Association on the best way to inspect your shingles. If your knees get a little wobbly when you climb a ladder, using binoculars is not a bad idea. Of course, you could ask two or three roofing contractors to take a look instead. But it is good policy to know something about the condition of your roof—and the language roofers use—before asking for estimates. The following chapter covers each type of roofing material in turn, from asphalt shingles to slate. But before getting into the particulars, it's worth taking time to nail down a few basic terms.

Roofing Speak

One square of shingles is the amount needed to cover 100 square feet of roof surface. This is the standard measure you'll find in contractor's estimates, and it is the way to order shingles and most other roofing materials. To cover that area you may need more of one type of shingle than another, depending on their size and configuration. But a square of standard asphalt shingles (the material most used on residences) is composed of three bundles of 27 shingles each.

Coverage refers to the number of layers of roofing protection provided. For example, standard modified bitumen for flat roofs, or asphalt shingles for sloped roofs, provide one layer. Dimensional asphalt shingles that show a more textured, shake-like roof, may provide two layers of coverage.

The slope of a roof is expressed as a ratio: inches of rise (vertically) per inches of run (horizontally). For example, a low-slope, 3-in-12 roof gains 3 inches of height every foot. On a 16-foot-long run from the eaves up to the ridge, the roof would rise 4 feet. Just measure a set distance along the side wall in from the eaves (run) and then a straight line up to the roof (rise) to find the slope on your roof. You could use slope to help calculate an order or to determine what type of roofing to use. For example, on standard asphalt shingle bundles you might read that the manufacturer doesn't recommend installation (or has special requirements) on roofs with a slope of less than 4-in-12.

As a safety guideline, you may use slope to decide if a roof is walkable. That means you can work on it without scaffolding. For most people, the cutoff point is a 6-in-12 slope, which means that a 16-foot-long run would rise 8 feet from the eaves to the ridge. But use some common sense too: for example, wear sneakers, and go up only when the roof is dry. And if you feel uneasy about being up there, even on a low-slope roof, stay on the ground.

Anatomy of a Roof

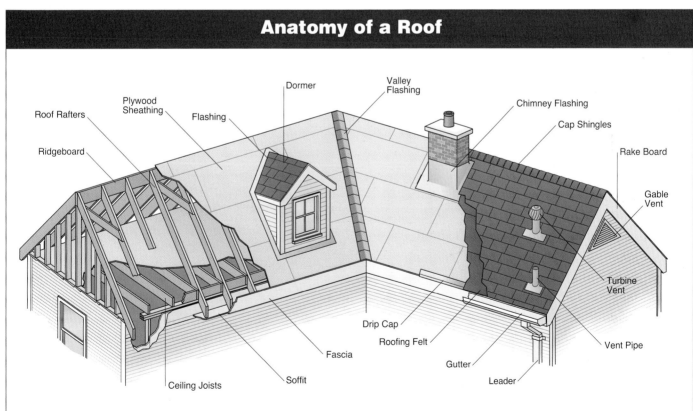

Roof Rafters · Plywood Sheathing · Flashing · Dormer · Valley Flashing · Chimney Flashing · Cap Shingles · Ridgeboard · Rake Board · Gable Vent · Turbine Vent · Drip Cap · Roofing Felt · Vent Pipe · Fascia · Gutter · Leader · Ceiling Joists · Soffit

The elements of most roofs are similar to those of the gable roof, shown above. Rafters carry the weight down to the house frame. Plywood sheathing supports water-shedding shingles. Flat roofs, the exception, have joists like floors instead of rafters.

Tools

Many of the tools needed for a roofing job are common to most households. There are some, however, that you probably need to pick up or rent. This chapter discusses the essential tools and equipment necessary for roofing and the wide variety of materials available.

Utility Knife

Carpenter's Level

Sliding T-Bevel

Claw Hammer

Measuring Tape

Hand Saw

Chalk-line Box

Folding Stick Rule

Saber Saw

Framing Square

Combination Square

Cordless Drill

Pop Riveter

Drill Bit Set

Work Gloves

Pry Bars

Circular Saw

Tin Snips

Working Up High

Working high above the ground is inevitable when repairing or replacing roofing and siding. Common sense, appropriate tools, and a few precautions get you through the job safely.

Choosing a Ladder

Use a ladder rated Type I (heavy duty, capable of bearing 250 pounds per rung). Wooden ladders are less likely to slide on a gutter or be blown over, and they do not conduct electricity. However, they are heavy and difficult to move without assistance. Aluminum ladders are easy to move, but they conduct electricity and may be blown down or knocked over. Expensive fiberglass ladders are relatively light and nonconductive. Make sure your ladder is at least 15 inches wide with rungs that are 12 inches apart. The best of them have nonskid feet and rope-and-pulley extension mechanisms. For eaves, gutter and fascia work, consider padded safety-wall grips.

Ladder Safety

Working on a ladder is inherently dangerous. Perhaps the biggest danger is becoming too comfortable. It's easy to become cavalier and try to reach just a little bit further to paint a spot without moving the ladder. Don't do it. Here are some other important things to consider when working on a ladder.

Getting the Correct Angle. The angle at which the ladder leans against the house is important. If the angle is too great, the ladder may be exposed to excessive strain and could break or bend. If the angle is too small, the ladder is likely to fall backward. Position the ladder so that the feet are 1 foot from the house for every 4 feet that the ladder runs from ground to contact point.

Leveling the Ladder. If the ground is so soft that a leg of the ladder might sink and cause it to tip to one side, set the ladder on a piece of plywood.

Extending the Ladder. Be sure the ladder extends 3 feet above the edge of the roof to permit a firm grip as you step onto the roof. Climb onto a roof from the eaves side only—never over a gable. Move the ladder frequently rather than trying to reach by leaning.

Climbing and Carrying

Always face forward and keep your hips within the rails of the ladder. Allow only one person on the ladder at a time. Bundles of shingles or rolls of roofing are best carried on one shoulder and steadied by one hand. Be wary of loose material on roofs, particularly wet leaves, loose granules, and detached shingles. Do not climb inclined roofs unless they are thoroughly dry. As a precaution, thoroughly sweep the area where you are working and wear shoes with rubber soles.

Caution: Always be aware of the location of electrical lines, particularly when moving a ladder. An aluminum or wet wooden ladder is conductive and can transmit a fatal shock.

Choosing a Ladder. Ladders must be at least 15 in. wide with 12 in. between rungs.

Getting the Correct Angle. Firemen use this quick method for determining the correct angle for leaning a ladder.

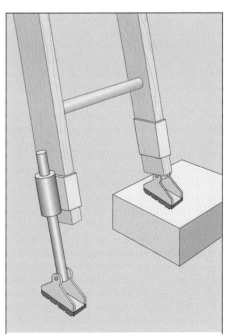

Leveling the Ladder. Make sure the feet of the ladder stand on a level surface. If necessary, shim the legs.

Choosing Cleats, Brackets, and Scaffolding

Adequate scaffolding and working platforms make a roofing or siding job easier and safer and can be rented for the duration of a job. They range from simple metal cleats to movable pump jacks that are raised or lowered.

Metal Cleats. Held by 16d nails hammered into the rafters where possible, metal cleats are placed beneath shingle tabs so nailholes can be sealed later. The cleats are installed at 6-foot intervals and hold a length of 2x4 that provides a working ledge. To remove the cleats, pull them out or firmly hammer the nail. Then coat the underside of the tab with roofing cement and press firmly.

Roof Brackets. Available in many forms, roof brackets attach to 16d nails that are hammered under shingles

and hold a plank working platform that can be moved as the job progresses.

Pump Jacks. These movable platform supports are raised and lowered to suit the task. When you pump the lever with your foot they ride up and down specially made steel rails or sets of doubled 2x4s. You can add accessory brackets to make a handy elevated workbench. Pump jacks also operate as freight elevators for raising large or heavy objects.

Ladder Jacks. Consider using ladder jacks for working under eaves or when applying siding. They are attached to the top of the ladder or slung underneath, and can support a 2x10 work platform up to 9 feet long.

Roof Brackets. With a plank set flat, roof brackets offer more room for tools and materials than metal cleats do.

Pump Jacks. This affordable type of scaffolding rides on special steel rails or doubled 2x4s set vertically.

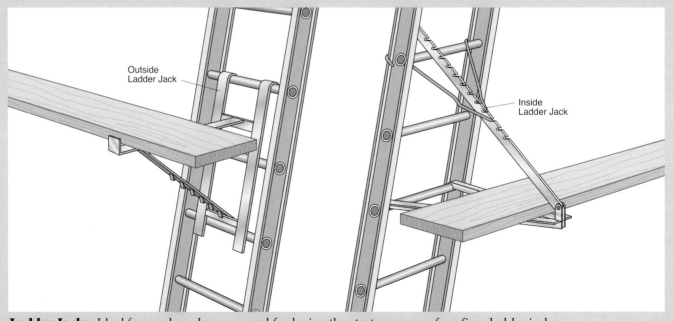

Outside Ladder Jack

Inside Ladder Jack

Ladder Jacks. Ideal for work under eaves and for laying the starter course of roofing, ladder jacks adjust with relative ease.

Roofing Materials

Composition Shingles

Composition shingles are relatively simple to apply, last 15 to 20 years, and come in a wide variety of colors, profiles and textures. These shingles, which are by far the most common roofing material in North America, are made with felt, wood fiber, or most typically these days, fiberglass mat impregnated with asphalt and coated with mineral granules. Most shingles have adhesive beneath the tabs to keep them from curling or blowing back. They are flexible and therefore adaptable, and can wrap almost all roof shapes and contours. They also suit every climate in North America.

Shingles can be applied to any roof that has a slope of 4 in 12 (4 inches of vertical rise for every 12 inches of horizontal run) or more. With double felt underlayment, they can be applied to a roof with a slope as low as 2 in 12 if shingle tabs are sealed down.

Often composition shingles are applied over an old roof of the same type. Three layers can be built up before all must be torn off (more than three layers are permissible only if the framing can bear the weight, and nails must be long enough to penetrate at least ¾ inch into the decking). If a tear-off is required, repair sheathing and remove all loose or protruding nails. Staples are used on new roofs and on roofs that have been stripped of old roofing.

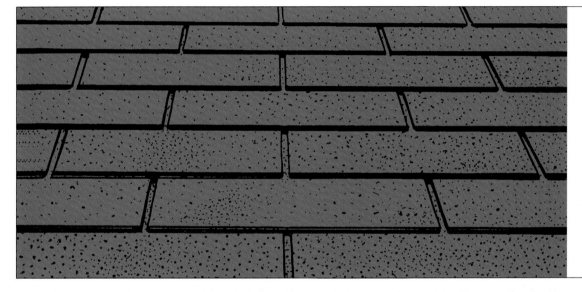

Composition Shingles. By far the most common roofing material in North America, composition shingles are relatively simple to apply, last 15 to 20 years or more, and are available in a wide variety of colors, profiles, and textures.

Types of Shingles

There are many styles of composition shingles. You can purchase them with three tabs that suggest three slate or wooden shingles, with two tabs, or strip shingles with no tabs. Also available are multi-layered textured shingles designed to look like wood shakes.

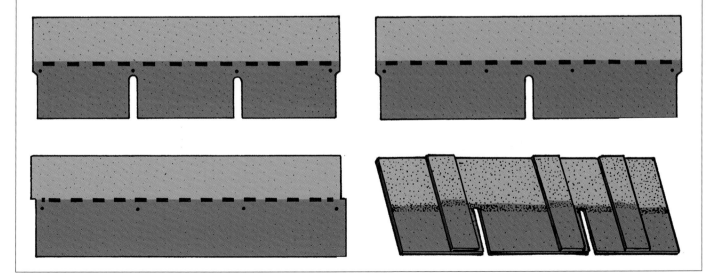

Roll Roofing

Ideal for porches with shallow slopes, garages, and utility buildings, roll roofing is quick and easy to apply. It is the least expensive option for roofs that have a very slight pitch. Roll roofing is not as attractive as composite shingles, but roofs with very shallow pitches are not visible from the ground anyway. One type of roll roofing, sometimes called selvage, is designed to be applied with a half-lap to provide double coverage. Selvage can be used with slopes as low as 1 in 12 (1 inch rise per 12 inches of run). Roll roofing is 36 inches wide and is available in a variety of colors. It can be applied with nails revealed (on slopes of 2 in 12 or more) or with nails covered by the roofing (on more shallow slopes).

Wood Shingles & Shakes

Among the most beautiful roofing materials are red cedar shingles and shakes. They have twice the insulation value of asphalt shingles, are lighter in weight than most other roofing materials, and are very resistant to hail damage. They also are well-suited to withstand the freeze-thaw conditions of variable climates. Wood shingles are machine cut and smoothed on both sides, while shakes are thicker and rough on at least one side. Pressure-injected fire retardant, as indicated by the industry designation "Certi-Guard," conforms to all state and local building codes for use in fire hazard regions. Given periodic coatings of wood preservative, shingles and shakes serve for 50 years or more. The drawbacks of using them include their high cost and slow application time.

Shakes differ from wood shingles in that they are split on one face and machine smoothed on the other. They vary in thickness and have a rustic, varied appearance. Because the rough surface of the split face sometimes allows water back under the shakes, a layer of underlayment (asphalt-saturated felt or fiberglass) is used between each course.

Both shingles and shakes require 1x4 sheathing spaced to suit the desired exposure. Along the roof rake and roof eaves 1x6 sheathing supports underlayment and seals the roof.

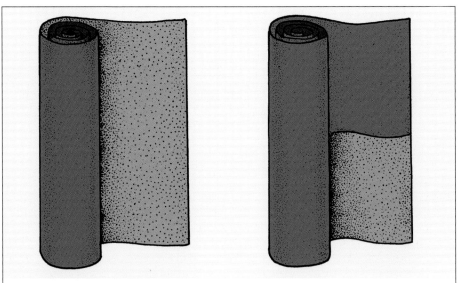

Roll Roofing. Roll roofing is 36 in. wide and comes in two types. One type has mineral granules covering the entire face and is applied with courses overlapping only 2 in. The other type, sometimes called selvage, has granules on only half its face. Roofing cement or hot asphalt is applied to the non-granule side, which is then covered with the next course of roofing. This double coverage roofing is for very slight pitches.

Wood Shingles and Shakes. Although quite simple, the installation of wood shingles and shakes is a time-consuming job.

Wood Fiber Shingle Panels

Another wood shingle option that is suitable for roofs with a 4-in-12 slope is hardboard shingle panels. With scored nailing and alignment lines to ease application, these shingles are installed in half the time it takes to apply cedar shakes. The panels do not crack with age and weather to a light gray. Shingle panels are 12 x 48 inches.

Wood Fiber Shingle Panels. A relatively new product, these panels install quickly and weather to a shingle-like gray.

Slate

Fireproof and extremely durable as well as beautiful, slate is among the oldest roofing materials available. Today it is also among the most expensive. In addition it requires spe-cial framing (designed to bear a heavier weight) and special furring. Difficult to cut and apply, slate roofing is definitely a job left to the professionals.

Composite Slate. Made of cement-impregnated non-asbestos fiber, synthetic slate looks like the real thing but weighs a lot less. Synthetic slate does not contain combustible materials and therefore carries the highest fire rating (Class A) from Underwriters Laboratories. Some

brands carry a warranty of 40 years. This is an expensive material. It typically is used on homes where historically appropriate materials are required. The material is difficult to cut and must be nailed carefully to avoid cracking the shingles. This is another job for experienced professionals.

Composite Slate. Cement-impregnated fiber creates a long-lasting imitation of the real thing.

Slate. One of the oldest roofing materials, slate is beautiful, long lasting, and very expensive.

Built-Up Roofing

Built-up roofing is suitable only for flat roofs and roofs with very slight pitches. For this reason it is used on many contemporary, flat-roofed homes and on slightly pitched porch roofs. Because it requires hot asphalt, a contractor must handle this job and the roof must have a minimum slope of ¼ inch per foot (no roof can have a slope of less than this anyway).

The oldest type of built-up roofing consists of several alternating layers of hot asphalt and felt. The final layer of asphalt is topped with pea gravel.

An increasingly common form of built-up roofing employs a large sheet of modified bitumen membrane to improve protection for flat or slightly sloped roofs. There are two types: plasticized, also called atacitic polypropylene (APP), and rubberized, also called styrene-butadiene-styrene (SBS). These relatively new materials are less prone to damage caused by ultra-violet rays. They have a higher melting point and therefore are slower to soften in direct sunlight. They also are more stable than roll roofing or felt. Because the application of plasticized roofing involves heating the bottom of the material with a propane torch, a contractor is required for the job. Granules or foil are added as a final layer for ultraviolet protection.

One advantage to using rubberized roofing is its ability to stretch in extreme temperatures. It may be heat welded, or applied with hot asphalt or a cold adhesive. Both rubberized and plasticized roofing benefit from a layer of fiberglass membrane for additional strength.

Metal Roofing

Widely used on commercial buildings, metal roofing is increasingly marketed for residential use. Depending on slope and framing, metal roofing can be installed over old roofing. It costs as much as three times more than conventional roofing but can last from 20 to 50 years with almost no maintenance. Unlike the old galvanized tin roofs, metal roofing today is made of steel with an alloy coating of aluminum and zinc. A wide spectrum of colors are available.

Many different profiles are available but the simple standing seam style (with overlapping ridges that run parallel to the eaves) is the most appropriate for older homes that might have had a tin roof at one time. This material usually requires professional application, and while the popularity of metal roofing is quickly increasing, a network of qualified residential contractors is only slowly developing.

Clay and Concrete Tile

Clay tile roofs, often used in the West, Southwest, and parts of the South, can last as long as the house itself. New fiber-reinforced concrete tiles, both flat and traditional barrel-shaped are less costly, easier to install, more uniform in appearance, and have most of the attributes of traditional tile. Beyond replacing cracked or missing tiles, the do-it-yourselfer probably will want to hire a professional for this difficult job.

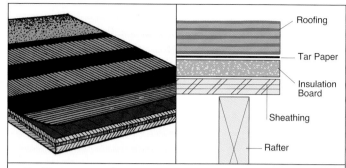

Built-Up Roofing. This material derives its name from the layers that combine to create a water-resistant surface. Pea gravel protects the roof from ultraviolet rays.

Metal Roofing. Metal roofing is making a comeback. With minimal maintenance it lasts up to 50 years.

Clay Tile. Traditional barrel-shape clay tiles complement Southwest architecture. The look is also available in tiles made of fiber-reinforced concrete. To maintain, replace cracked or missing tiles.

Synthetic Roofing

This new generation of steep-slope roofing products uses rubber and plastics combined with additives such as colorants, fire retardants, and UV inhibitors to mimic the look of natural slate, wood shakes, and wood shingles. There are a number of products available, and they are all manufactured differently. For example, some products include glass fibers, limestone, or cellulose as part of their formulations. Some contain recycled materials; others do not. But most can be recycled at the end of the shingle's life.

When compared with natural slate, these products are much lighter in weight and are less expensive. They can be installed over a standard roof deck without the need for additional support. They are also easier to cut and install than slate. Products may vary, but synthetic roofing can carry a Class A fire rating and a UL Class 4 impact resistance rating, which is the highest rating for a roofing product. Many products offer a 50-year warranty.

Synthetic Roofing. Consisting of engineered polymers and other ingredients, these products are formed to look like natural slate, top, wood shakes, above, and wood shingles. Some products contain recycled material.

Energy Star Roofs

The type of roof you select can have a significant impact on your energy costs, especially your cooling costs. A roofing material that reflects the sun's heat can help reduce air conditioning costs and help prolong the life of the roof. The federal government's Energy Star program qualifies roofing materials based on the reflectivity of the materials. Reflectivity is measured on a scale from 0 to 1, with 1 being the most reflective. For steep-slope roofs, products must have an initial reflectivity of 0.25 or greater. Three years after installation, the product's reflectivity must be 0.15 or greater. For a list of approved products, go to energystar.gov.

Concrete Tile. Concrete tile roofs require special framing and expert installation. Repairs are within the skill of the do-it-yourselfer, but whole roof installation is still left to the professionals.

prep & flashing

Tear-Off or Reroof?

A reroofing job consists of applying new roofing material over the existing surface. This is less expensive and easier than a "tear-off" job, which requires that the old roofing be stripped off and hauled away.

Old tile and slate roofs cannot be covered over. Because they are heavy and impossible to nail through, they must be torn off. Roll roofing placed over any other surface (even shingles) is unsightly. If the house can take another layer of roofing, make sure there is a sound foundation for nailing and an even surface for the new shingles.

1 Counting the Layers. The first step in determining whether or not you can reroof is to check the rake of the roof to determine how many roofing layers exist. The rake is the sloped edge of the roof. Remember that drip edge sometimes is applied before reroofing and may hide evidence of previous layers. Once the number of layers is determined, check local roofing codes for the maximum number of roofing layers allowed. The answer varies depending on the type of roofing materials and the pitch of the roof. For wood shingles, codes typically allow the original roof plus one reroof. For asphalt shingles, codes typically allow the original plus two reroofs. Ask your local building inspector for specifics.

2 Checking for Solid Sheathing. All rotten boards under the old roofing must be replaced. Go into the attic and examine all suspicious spots including voids and separating plywood. Check for rot by poking with a screwdriver. If the rot is limited to a few places, you need only remove the old roofing and replace the boards in those spots. If necessary, build up the roofing above the replacement sheathing with extra layers of shingles to make a flush surface for the new roof.

3 Checking Surface Conditions. Do not expect the new roofing to smooth over dips and waves found in the old roofing. If the surface of the old roofing is not uniformly flat, it must be removed. Shake roofs, shingle roofs that have curled excessively, and old-style interlocking shingles must be torn off.

Caution: If you reroof when a tear-off is called for, the results may include costly structural damage to your home and possible fines for violating local codes.

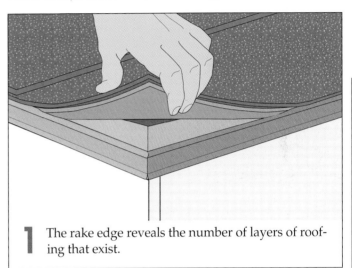

1 The rake edge reveals the number of layers of roofing that exist.

2 Check between rafters for any signs of deterioration of the sheathing.

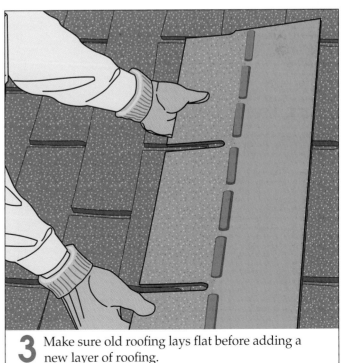

3 Make sure old roofing lays flat before adding a new layer of roofing.

1. Before roofing over old shingles, strip a few sections down to the deck to check the decking for water damage.

2. Use a pry bar to pry off the old ridge cap. A new ridge cap will need to be installed over the new layer of shingles.

3. The new layer needs a level surface; broken or bent tabs must be replaced. Cut them away with a sharp utility knife.

4. Cut a tab from a new shingle, and nail it in place with two or three roofing nails to fill the space in the existing roof.

5. Scrape away old roof tar around plumbing vent stacks to clear the way for a new piece of molded flashing.

6. Install new flashing made from molded plastic or metal over the new roofing. The top edge will be shingled.

Tear-Off Techniques

Removing an old roof is a matter of hard physical work, and although no special skills are required, a bit of planning and preparation makes the job less difficult.

Tearing-off creates a massive amount of debris, so plan ahead by calling several dumpster rental companies to get the best price. If you tell them the square footage of the roof and the number of roofing layers that are to be torn off, they can estimate the size and number of containers needed. Choose the location for the dumpster carefully, minimizing damage to landscaping and limiting carrying distance as much as possible.

Warn your neighbors ahead of time and get their permission if you need to place the dumpster on their property. Place dropcloths wherever debris is likely to fall; nails and broken shingles wreak havoc with the lawn mower. If you are lucky, the shingles may come off in large groups. (This indicates that they were not nailed down properly.) Usually shingles come off two or three at a time.

1 Starting at the Top. Begin at the ridge, and work your way down. (This is especially important for wood shingles so debris does not fall through the open sheathing.) Tear off wood shingles or shakes by sliding a crowbar or prybar underneath and pulling sharply upward. This loosens several rows at a time.

2 Saving Old Flashing. Remove flashing carefully so it can be used as a template for new flashing. If old shingles and nails are removed with care, the flashing can be reused. In the case of chimney flashing where the upper part may be embedded in mortar, you may be able to carefully bend the flashing out of the way rather than go through the trouble to remove it.

3 Inspecting the Deck. Once you have removed the old roofing, inspect all of the sheathing and replace broken or rotten pieces with a material of the same thickness. On older homes the sheathing may be $7/8$ inch to 1 inch thick. Plywood sheathing is not available in thicknesses greater than $3/4$ inch. Use extra layers of felt or roofing materials to make up the difference.

Tear-Off Techniques. If the dumpster sits in a public access area, rope off the area and provide signs in accordance with local ordinances.

1 Use a crowbar to tear off shingles, working from the ridge downward.

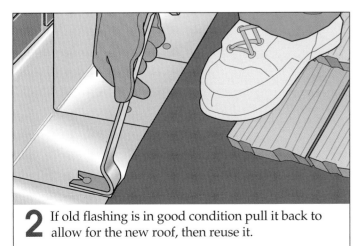

2 If old flashing is in good condition pull it back to allow for the new roof, then reuse it.

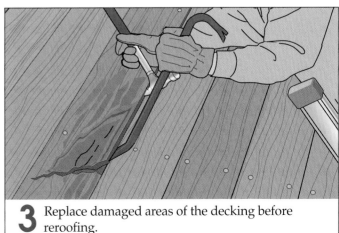

3 Replace damaged areas of the decking before reroofing.

Roof Sheathing

Sheathing stabilizes the roof and provides a nailing surface for the roofing material. Roof sheathing can be ⅜ inch (only for 16-inch on-center rafters) or ½ inch thick (for 16- or 24-inch-on-center rafters). There's not much cost difference. When making repairs, use panels that are the same thickness as the originals. Plywood is the choice sheathing material, but your building code may allow less expensive nonveneer sheathing materials like oriented-strand board (OSB). Whether you use plywood or OSB, be sure the panels are APA-rated Exposure 1 where you'll enclose the soffit. For open soffits, use panels marked Exterior or Exposure 1 of the appropriate grade to permit painting or staining. Be sure to stagger the sheathing-panel joints so the seams don't line up.

Prolonged exposure to the weather can damage the framing, so waterproof the structure as soon as possible.

Use caution: the greater the roof slope, the more hazardous the job. On steep roofs, nail down 2x4 cleats for footing support as you work up the roof.

Make the Sheathing Layout. For new roofs, draw a scaled sheathing layout for the entire roof on paper, showing panel sizes, placement, and number of panels; graph paper is easiest to use. Plan any panel cutting on one side so you can use the cut-off portions on the opposite side. You can start at the eaves with a full 4-foot-wide panel, provided you don't end up at the top having to use a strip less than 16 inches wide. A narrow strip may be too weak to support a person or provide a solid backing for the roofing. Trim the panels of the first row to adjust the width of the last row. Stagger the panels in succeeding rows so the ends fall on different framing members. The sketch will reveal the number of panels required.

Making the Sheathing Layout

1. Plan for sheathing installation by drawing a scaled layout of panel placement.

2. Start from a bottom corner of the roof, and use panel clips where rafters are placed 24 in. on center.

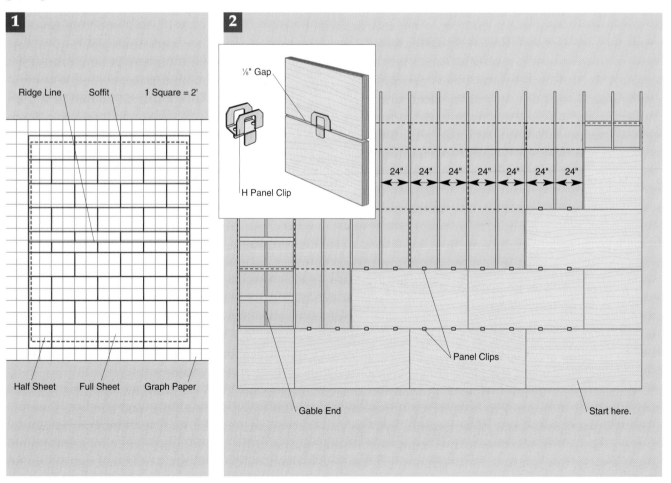

1

Ridge Line   Soffit   1 Square = 2'

Half Sheet   Full Sheet   Graph Paper

2

⅛" Gap

H Panel Clip

24" 24" 24" 24" 24" 24" 24"

Panel Clips

Gable End

Start here.

1. To allow for a fascia to be nailed across the rafter tails, the bottommost course of roof sheathing should be installed so that its top edge does not protrude past the rafter's tail cut.

2. Begin installation at a bottom corner, placing the long side perpendicular to the rafters, with the end joint over the center of a rafter. Use 8d nails every 6 in. along the edges and 12 in. in the field.

3. To support the panel seams where they fall between rafters, use plywood panel clips in the center of the joint.

Insert one end onto an installed sheet, and slide the next sheet onto the support.

4. Start the second course with a half (4 x 4-ft.) panel so that the seams will not fall in the same places. Stagger the panel ends on several different rafters as you work up the roof.

5. Mark the plywood at the eaves and ridge, and snap a chalk line to help guide nailing into the centers of the rafters. If you miss a rafter, pull the nail so that it won't work up into the shingles.

Roof Flashing

To keep the roof watertight you need to install flashing at many seams. Place it around vent pipes, chimneys and skylights, in open-style valleys that connect two sections of roof, where the roof meets a side of the building, and on the ends of eaves and rakes.

Flashing can be made from galvanized sheet steel, aluminum, copper, or flexible plastic in some cases. Generally you need to use nails made of the same material as the flashing. Copper nails may be hard to find, but you should use them if you are going to be installing copper flashing. Other metals may cause chemical reactions which might undermine the strength of the copper and eventually cause leaks.

Drip Edge

Drip edge covers the ends of eaves and rakes, which often need to be protected by more than just the overhang of the roofing material. Install preformed drip flashing along the eaves of the roof before you place the underlayment (generally felt paper) and along rakes on each side after the underlayment is down.

Cut the corners carefully and wear gloves, as cut sheet metal is extremely sharp. Nail the drip edge to the roof sheathing every 8 to 10 inches. Do not nail the drip edge to the fascia.

Vent Collars

Projections through the roof, such as plumbing vent pipes, are best sealed with flashing sleeves. These sleeves are available in a variety of styles and materials, including lead, sheet metal, rubber, and plastic. The most modern type (it's also the easiest to install) has a flexible rubber collar that makes a tight seal around the pipe. Below the collar, a piece of metal flashing makes the watertight connections to the roof. On the high side,

the flashing tucks under shingles. On the low side, it rests on top of them. You can trim shingles to make a neat fit around the flashing.

Step Flashing

Step flashing joins shingles to the sloping side of a wall or a chimney. Step flashing requires that each piece of flashing overlaps the one below it. The flashing is interlaced with the shingles as well. You can purchase step flashing precut, or you can cut the flashing into shingle-like pieces 10 inches long and 2 inches wider than the exposure of the roofing. You have to remember to insert a piece at the end of every course of shingles. You nail the high side against the adjacent structure, such as a dormer where it will be covered by siding, but do not nail the low side on the roof.

Valley Flashing

Valley flashing is installed on top of the sheathing and felt paper but beneath the roofing. The two basic types of valley treatments are called open and closed. If the flashing material is visible after the roof is finished, it is considered open. If the roofing material covers or even replaces the flashing, it is considered closed.

Open flashing works for all types of roofs. On the other hand, closed flashing is used only with asphalt shingles that are flexible enough to be woven together across the angle created by a valley.

Valley flashing should extend 6 inches or more on each side of the valley centerline. (For low-sloped roofs, make that 10 inches.) Valley flashing can be galvanized steel or aluminum, center-crimped or painted. (If you crimp the flashing after it is painted, retouch the paint at the crimp line.) When you are using cedar roofing, underlay valley metal with 15-pound builder's felt (minimum). Double-coverage with a strip of felt paper or heavier roll roofing is a good idea for backup protection under all open valleys.

Types of Flashing

Nail drip edge along the rakes and eaves before installing your first course of shingles.

Vents are best sealed with formed flashing. A rubber vent collar seals the pipe.

Step flashing is short angled pieces of flashing that seal between shingles and walls.

Counterflashing is sealed into mortar to cover the top edge of standard flashing below.

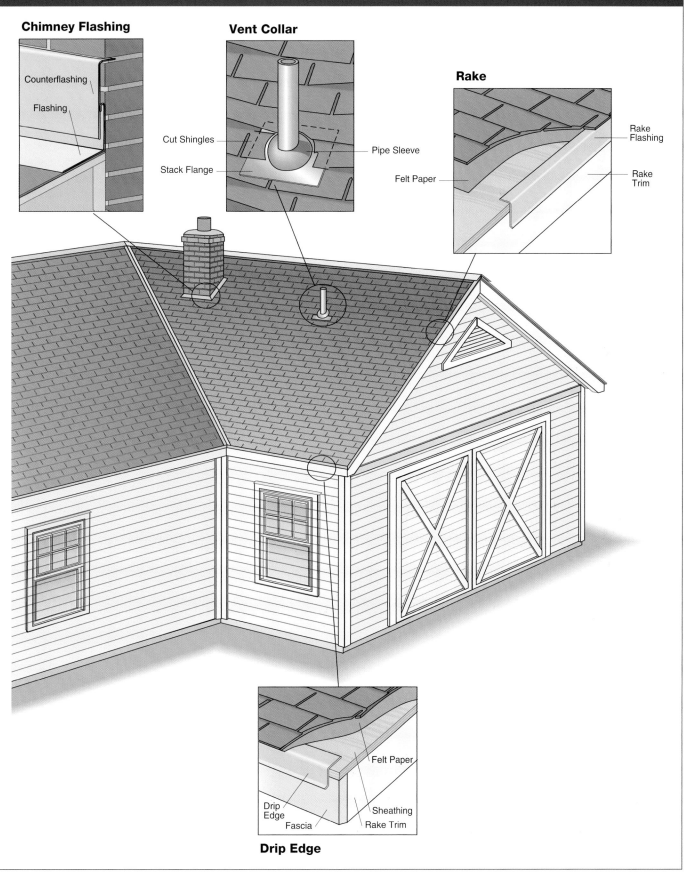

Chimney Flashing

Counterflashing

Flashing

Vent Collar

Cut Shingles

Stack Flange

Pipe Sleeve

Rake

Rake Flashing

Felt Paper

Rake Trim

Drip Edge

Felt Paper

Drip Edge

Fascia

Sheathing

Rake Trim

The ends of eaves and rakes often need to be protected by more than just the overhang of the roofing material. Install preformed eaves and rake flashing (called drip edge) along the eaves before underlayment is applied and along rakes after the underlayment is down. Cut corners carefully with tin snips, both for the sake of appearance and for better coverage. Nail the drip edge to the roof sheathing every 8 to 10 inches. Do not nail the drip edge to the fascia.

Wrap-around end-cap flashing covers the edges of old roofing layers. Be sure flashing overlaps at corners. For example, rake flashing must overlap eaves flashing so water is shed downward without working its way beneath the flashing **(A)**.

For roofing trimmed flush with the fascia, this type of **end-cap** covers the edges of layers and keeps water and ice from backing under the old shingles **(B)**.

A **canted drip edge** of this variety carries the water away from the fascia **(C)**.

This type of **drip edge** is designed to contain pea gravel on a built-up roof **(D)**.

Sometimes called **drip cap,** this flashing adds a lip to the roof edge that overlaps the gutter **(E).**

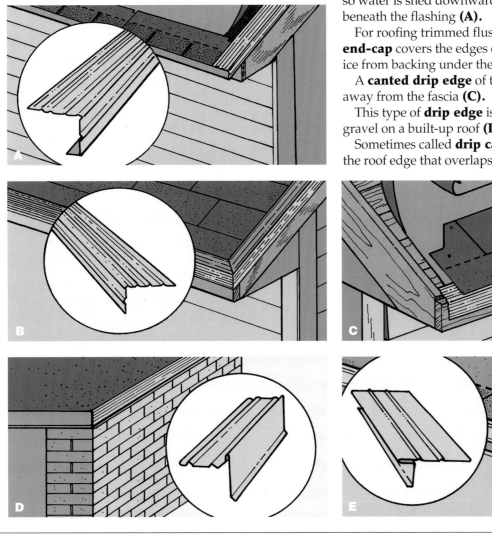

Flashing is available in a variety of forms, starting with aluminum coil on the least expensive end of the spectrum and copper sheeting on the most expensive end. Aluminum is readily available in widths ranging from 10 to 36 inches. Colors vary as well with the most typical being white, black, and brown. W-bend galvanized steel flashing (right) is available in 8- to 10-foot lengths, 20 to 24 inches wide. If you would like to bend the flashing for a custom fit, rent a break (a device typically used to neatly bend aluminum siding soffits and trim). They are simple to use and available at most rental shops.

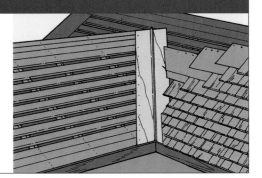

Applying Flashing

Flashing is applied in places where regular roofing materials cannot prevent leaks. It is found around vent pipes, chimneys and skylights, and also is used in valleys that connect two sections of roof, in places where the roof meets a side of the house, and on the ends of eaves and rakes. Flashing is made of galvanized sheet metal, aluminum or copper. Roofing cement is used in conjunction with flashing but cement alone can't do the job. If the original flashing did its job well, use it as a guide for applying new pieces. Keep sections of the old flashing for templates and install the new flashing in the same place and manner as the old. If the old flashing leaked and you cannot locate the source of the problem, it is best to call in a professional.

The nails used must be made of the same material as the flashing. A mixture of aluminum, tin, steel, or copper may cause corrosion or discoloration.

If you find that the roof suffered from blistering, wore out prematurely, had an exceptional number of buckled shingles, and you find evidence of moisture damage in rafters or attic insulation, it may be an indication that the roof needs additional vents. In the case of roof vents, the rule of thumb is one square foot of ventilating area per 150 square feet of attic space. If you determine that the roof needs additional vents, now is the time to install them.

Valley Flashing

Valley flashing is installed on top of the underlayment, but beneath the roofing. The two basic types of valley treatments are called open and closed. If the flashing material is visible after the roof is finished it is considered open. If the roofing material covers the flashing it is considered closed. Open flashing works for all types of roofs. On the other hand, closed flashing is used only for composition shingles. Open valleys are essential for wooden shingles, slate, and tile because the nature of materials do not allow them to overlap to make a closed valley. Open valleys also are commonly used with asphalt shingles that have metal or roll roofing flashing. Open valley flashing is the more complicated to apply, but provides greater protection, especially from torrential downpours and the slow melt of heavy snow.

Installing Open Valley Flashing

If you are reroofing a roof that has open flashing be certain that the old flashing will last as long as the new roof. If not, you may have to remove the old flashing by cutting out a section of the old roofing wide enough to allow its removal. Install new flashing and fill in the remaining space with roofing material.

W-Bend Metal. For open valleys it is preferable to use preformed W-bend metal (page 24, so called because in profile it looks somewhat like the letter W). This type of flashing has a ridge bent in the middle to prevent water from rushing down one roof slope and under the shingles on the other slope.

In an open valley the exposed portion of the flashing is wider at the bottom than at the top to allow better drainage. On either side of the valley, snap chalk lines that begin 6 inches apart at the top and widen at the rate of about $\frac{1}{8}$ inch per foot as they descend.

Waterproofing Shingle Underlayment

A roof depends on gravity to make water run down and off, but when held back by ice, or during intense driving rain, water can work its way up and under even properly installed shingles. Because normal felt underlayment is not completely waterproof, especially around nailholes, water can work its way in. For those who experience harsh winters, it's reassuring to know you can install additional insurance against water damage.

Waterproof shingle underlayment is a special material made of asphalt and elastic polymers designed to adhere tightly to roof sheathing and around the shanks of nails driven through it. This self-sealing attribute ensures that water cannot get past it, even where you drive a nail.

Install the underlayment along those areas where ice dams and driving rain can create a problem, or where water tends to accumulate: along the eaves, around skylights, in valleys, in saddles, or on low-pitched roofs. Normal felt underlayment should still be installed in non-critical areas, and metal flashing should still be used, as per ordinary roof installation.

Waterproofing shingle underlayment must be installed over bare sheathing. Installation is a two-man job. Unroll the underlayment while your assistant peels off the plastic film backing. Carefully set the material in place. During installation, the material is slightly tacky, but can be lifted and repositioned if necessary. However, once it's installed and exposed to sunlight, the underlayment locks tight.

It's important to know what waterproof shingle underlayment can and cannot do. The underlayment will protect those vulnerable areas of your roof from leaks; it does not prevent the formation of the ice dams that form those leaks. Proper insulation and ventilation of your attic are essential to avoid ice damming in the first place. In addition, because the underlayment is a complete vapor barrier, it can prevent the escape of moisture from your attic. To prevent condensation-related problems, make sure that your attic is adequately ventilated.

Roll Roofing Valleys

A less costly and less durable option for open valleys is roll roofing. Typically used with asphalt shingles, two layers of roll roofing are applied: One layer is 18 inches wide (the full width of the roll cut lengthwise in half) and one is 36 inches wide (full width). The 18-inch piece is laid granule side down while the 36-inch piece is laid granule side up. Strike a chalk line down the center of each piece to center it in the valley. Nail one side only at first. Before nailing the other side, press the roofing firmly into the valley to eliminate voids that might become punctured later. Mark the valley with chalk lines 6 inches apart at the top of the valley. The bottom is 6 inches wide plus ⅛ inch per foot of descent. The shingles overlap the chalk line and later are trimmed. The uppermost corner of the shingle is nipped diagonally to direct water flow into the valley. A final dab of roofing cement applied after shingles are trimmed keeps water from working under the roofing.

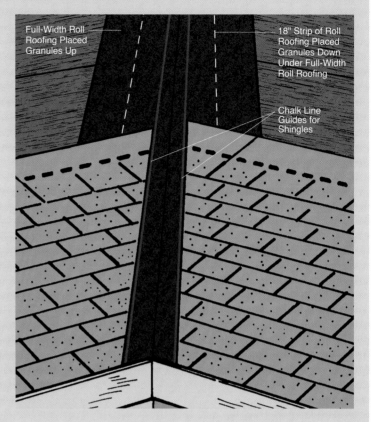

Full-Width Roll Roofing Placed Granules Up

18" Strip of Roll Roofing Placed Granules Down Under Full-Width Roll Roofing

Chalk Line Guides for Shingles

Installing Roll Roofing Valleys. Two layers of roll roofing, one 18 in. wide, the other 36 in. wide, make a nonmetallic valley for use with composition shingles.

Closed Valley Flashing

An extra layer of underlayment is placed in a closed valley. For added protection in harsh climates add a 24-inch-wide sheet of aluminum or galvanized metal. Shingles are laid over the flashing in an alternating fashion or they are half-laced (trimmed down the center of the valley where one plane of shingles overlaps the other).

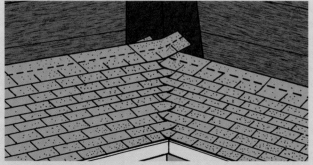

Installing Closed Valley Flashing. Such a valley is woven (or laced) together with courses from either side of the valley alternately overlapping each other. Each overruns the valley by at least a tab and a half.

Half-Laced Valley

The half-laced (sometimes called half-woven) valley is another type of closed valley. One layer of roofing overlaps the other and is trimmed instead of woven. The overlap is put on the face of the roof that bears the most water. The bottom layer of shingles overlaps the valley by at least 12 inches. After trimming, adhere the topmost layer with roofing cement.

Installing a Half-Laced Valley. The half-laced valley is a type of closed valley. The overlap is put on the face of the roof that bears the most water. Nails are kept at least 6 in. from the center of the valley.

Installing Continuous Flashing

Use this simple type of flashing only in places where the joint is horizontal. For example, the joint at which the front wall of a dormer meets the roof, or where a shed roof is attached to a wall. Lay your last course of roofing so that the tops of the shingles butt the wall. If necessary, adjust the exposures in the last two courses so the last course, which will be trimmed to butt the wall, is at least 8 inches long.

1 Bending Flashing. Continuous flashing is bent to match the angle of the joint to be covered. Position the bend so that there will be at least 5 inches of flashing on the wall and 4 inches on the roof. Use clamps and boards to bend the metal. Alternately you can rent a break (typically used to form aluminum soffits and trim caps) to custom-bend aluminum flashing. (It does not work for galvanized steel.)

2 Attaching the Flashing. Put roofing cement on the last course of shingles. On walls that have wood siding, slip the the flashing behind the siding and then press it into the cement. You don't need to nail the flashing to the wall. Nail the flashing to the roof deck with roofing nails every 2 or 3 feet.

3 Covering the Flashing. Cut the tabs off as many shingles as you need for the course. Coat the flashing with roofing cement. Press the tabs into the roofing cement leaving gaps between each that approximate the cutouts between tabs on an intact shingle. Tabs cut from a standard shingle will cover the flashing plus about 1 inch more. Do not nail the tabs. Use a caulk gun to apply a bead of roofing cement along the flashing junction.

1 Score the flashing material, and sandwich it at the bending point between two 1x4s.

2 Siding overlaps flashing so that water sheds downward on top of, not under, the flashing.

3 Cut tabs off shingles, and press them into roofing cement applied to the flashing.

Flashing Brick or Stucco

If the wall is masonry or stucco, the job is more difficult because the flashing must be set into the wall.

1 Bending Lip on Flashing. Using two boards, clamp the sheet metal or aluminum flashing so that ½ inch protrudes freely over the edge. Use a hammer to bend that same ½ inch of flashing so that it sticks up at a 90-degree angle.

2 Cutting the Slot. Use a piece of chalk to mark a line about 5 inches above the roof. Use the nearest mortar line if it is a masonry wall. Then use a circular saw (with a masonry blade) or a chisel to cut a ½-inch-deep slot along that line. Bend the flashing a second time so that it fits on the roof.

3 Sealing with Mortar. Stuff the slot with mortar or silicone caulk, and press the top lip of the flashing into the slot.

1 Score a line on the flashing, and bend the lip as shown.

2 Open the mortar line using a chisel or circular saw with a masonry blade.

3 Fill the chiseled mortar lines with mortar or caulk, and set the flashing in place.

Vents and soil stacks are covered with sleeves. A flap at the base of the sleeve makes a waterproof seal. These sleeves are available in a variety of styles and materials including lead, sheet metal, rubber, and plastic (right). All types are easy to install.

Shingle up to the base of the vent or stack. Cut the shingle around the stack, apply roofing cement and slip on the sleeve (below left).

Shingles overlap the upper half of the vent sleeve. Cut the overlapping courses around the stack, leaving a ½-inch gap. Cement the tabs to the sleeve (below right).

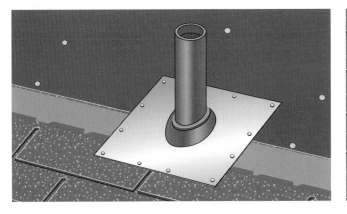

Step Flashing

Use step flashing on a shingled roof where the roof meets the sloping side of a wall or a chimney. (For roll or panel roofing use continuous flashing.) Step flashing requires that each piece of flashing overlaps the one below it. The flashing is interlaced with the shingles as well. You can purchase step flashing precut, or you can cut the flashing into shingle-like pieces 10 inches long and 2 inches wider than the exposure of the roofing. For example, if the shingle exposure is 5 inches, each shingle is cut 10 x 7 inches. Install the flashing so that it has the same exposure as the shingles, nailing the the top edge into the roof only so the nails are covered by shingles.

In the illustrations at right, the roofing exposure (the amount of roofing material visible in each course) is 5 inches.

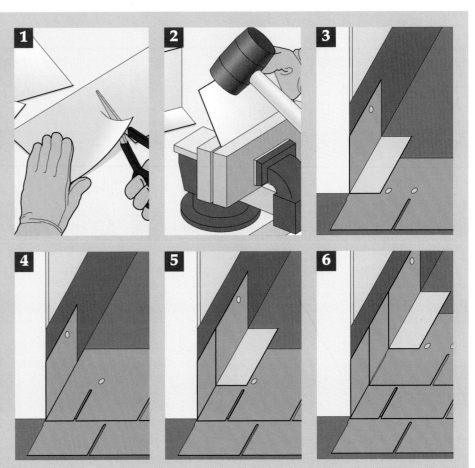

Chimney Flashing

This job is probably the most complicated part of roofing a house. Old flashing pieces can be used as templates, but keep in mind that by reroofing or tearing off the old roof, the dimensions of the flashing have changed. Chimney flashing typically consists of base flashing (which wraps the front of the chimney), step flashing (which is placed up the sides of the chimney), cricket flashing (a peaked piece that diverts water from the upslope side of the chimney) and pieces of counter flashing (also called cap flashing, which hangs over all the other flashing pieces).

If the chimney is 24 inches or wider, construct a cricket along the upper side of the chimney. This helps keep water and snow from building up in this critical area.

Before flashing, complete all final roofing up to the base of the chimney and no further. All metal flashing must be at least 26-gauge (0.019-inch, or 0.48mm)

corrosion-resistant coil stock (either aluminum or copper). In some cases, you will weave metal step flashing with the shingles.

For chimneys and skylights, install apron flashing over the shingles (below left); then continue with the step flashing. Install a section of flashing, then a shingle, and so on. You finish with another apron on the up-roof side, which goes under the shingles. Step flashing pieces are rectangular, usually 10 inches long and 2 inches wider than the exposed face of the roofing shingles. Fold the 10-inch length in half so that it can extend 5 inches onto the roof deck and 5 inches up the chimney, skylight, or wall. For chimneys, install cap flashing about 1½ inches into the mortar joints of the chimney; bend it over to cover the step flashing. Then you install a roof-like cricket on the up-roof side (below right), and cover it with roll roofing.

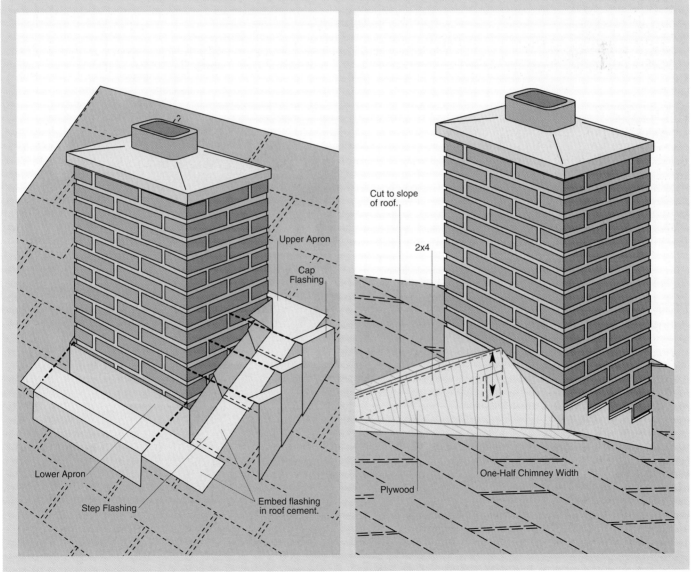

Upper Apron

Cap Flashing

Lower Apron

Step Flashing

Embed flashing in roof cement.

Cut to slope of roof.

2x4

Plywood

One-Half Chimney Width

asphalt shingles

Selecting Composition Shingles

Shingles are purchased by the square, which is enough shingles to cover 100 square feet at the recommended exposure. Shingles typically are packaged 80 to the square, though larger shingles are packaged 64 to the square. Each square is made up of bundles of paper-wrapped blocks of shingles. Most squares are made up of three bundles, but heavier squares are made up of four.

The durability of shingles used to be rated by the weight of the square. The heavier the square, the thicker and longer-lived the shingle. Today shingles are given lifetime ratings of 15, 20, and 25 years. Prices rise accordingly. Colors include white, black, and shades of brown, green, gray, and blue. Pressed texture and granule coloration combine to produce shingles that resemble wood shingles and shakes.

When selecting a color, remember that roofs last 20 years, far longer than the latest fashion trends. Neutral blacks, whites, and grays remain the most popular colors.

Composition shingles can be applied to any roof that has a slope of 4 in 12 (4 inches rise for every 12 inches of run) or more. With double felt underlayment, they can be applied to a roof with a slope as low as 2 in 12 if shingle tabs are sealed down.

Deciding to Reroof

Composition shingles are a versatile material and can be used to cover almost anything that accepts a nail.

Composition Shingles. Nail down warped shingles and fill voids. Usually only two or three layers of shingles are allowed; check your local codes.

Wood Shingles. Add thin, beveled strips (sometimes called horse feathers) to fill the voids between courses, and notch in 1x4s at the rakes and eaves to create a smooth platform for a new layer of roofing.

Roll Roofing. If the slope is at least 4 in 12, roll roofing makes a smooth bed for a new layer of composition shingles. Remove all loose nails before reroofing.

Tile and Slate Roofs. Tile and slate roofs, as well as metal and fiberglass panels, are impossible to nail through and therefore cannot be reroofed with composition shingles. Shakes are too uneven to take new roofing and must be removed as well.

Different Types of Composition Shingles

Composition shingles come in a variety of styles and colors to complement the architectural and color scheme of your house. Here are three of the most common composition shingle styles you will find.

    Standard Three-Tab Shingles. These are the most common style in North America today. They typically are sold 80 shingles per square, three bundles per square (left).

Shadow Line Tab Shingles. The illusion of thickness and a slate-like appearance are created by a line of darkened granules. These too come 80 shingles per square, three bundles per square (center).

    Mock Wood Shakes. Added thickness and the use of color give mock wood shingles their wood-like appearance. Because they are thicker and heavier, they are sold only 64 shingles per square, four bundles per square (right).

Estimating Materials on Gabled Roofs

You need to be able to tell your local lumberyard or roofing supplier how many squares (100 square feet) of roofing you need. By determining the square footage of your roof and adding 10 percent for ridges and waste, you can estimate costs and order materials. It is safest and most convenient to take as many measurements as you can from the ground. With a simple gable roof, you can take all the measurements without a ladder. But you'll have to climb up to directly measure details such as dormers. Here's how to measure your roof with little or no climbing:

1 **Sketching the Roof.** From the ground make a rough sketch of your roof. Include all planes of the roof including valleys, dormers, and chimneys. Do not worry about getting it to scale. Next, reduce the diagram to a series of triangles, rectangles, and squares, drawing in dotted lines where appropriate. (Later these shapes are calculated for area.)

2 **Measuring Gable and Eaves Lengths.** First measure the length of your house on one of the eave sides. Include the gable overhang in your measurement. To determine how far the overhangs protrude, stand directly under them and measure to the house. This will give you a rough measurement of the length of the eave that's close enough for estimating materials. Mark the eave length on your drawing.

Now measure the width of the gable end, again including overhangs. Jot down this measurement, but don't put it on the drawing yet.

3 **Measuring Slope.** The purpose of the next two steps is to determine the length of the rake, which is one sloped edge of your roof. When you know the length of the rake and the length of the eaves, you can multiply them to get the square footage of your roof.

First, calculate the slope of the roof. Slope is expressed as inches of roof rise (unit rise) per 12 inches of roof run (unit run). A 6-in-12 roof rises 6 inches per 12 inches of run. The slope of the roof is determined from the ground by using a spirit level and a ruler. Mark the level 12 inches from one end. Stand back from a gable, and hold the level so that one end appears to touch the eaves. Make sure the level is exactly horizontal. At the 12-inch mark on the level, hold the ruler upright and note the number of inches to the rake. This is the rise. Almost all house slopes are expressed in whole inches. For example, 4 in 12, 6 in 12, etc.

4 **Determining Total Rise.** Let us say for example that the gable end of your house is 20 feet wide including the overhangs. That means the base of the triangle

you are calculating, or the total run of the roof, is 10 feet long. Let us also assume you have determined that the slope is 6 in 12. This means that in a total run of 10 feet, the roof rises 5 feet.

5 **Calculating Rake Length.** This is an opportunity to put your high school geometry to use. Remember the Pythagorean theorem? This useful formula asserts that if you know the measurements of two sides of a right triangle, the third can be computed. This means that if you know the length of a gable (which you measured from the ground) and you know its height, you can determine the length of the rake.

The total rise squared times the total run squared gives us the length of the rake squared. In our example, the 10-foot total run squared equals 100. The 5-foot total rise squared equals 25. Added together they equal 125, which is the rake squared. The square root of 125 is 11.18, so the rake is 11 feet $2\frac{1}{8}$ inches long. Now multiply the rake length by the length of the eaves. Then you have the area of one side on the gable roof.

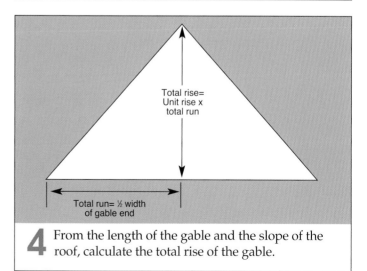

1 To determine the area of the roof, sketch a simple bird's-eye view. Divide the plan into squares, rectangles, and triangles.

Total rise= Unit rise x total run

Total run= ½ width of gable end

4 From the length of the gable and the slope of the roof, calculate the total rise of the gable.

6 Calculating the Area. If you are dealing with a simple gable roof with no dormers, just double the area of one side of the roof and add 10 percent for waste and ridge cap shingles. Divide the square footage by 100 for the total number of squares needed. If your rake is 11.18 feet long and your eave end is 40 feet long, one side of your roof will be 447.2 square feet. Both sides will be 894.4 square feet. You need nine squares to cover the roof. Adding 10 percent, you should order 10 squares.

If you have dormers, climb up on the roof and measure their length and width directly. When all measurements are determined, compute the area of each roof plane using the following formulas: One side of a rectangle or square multiplied by an adjacent side yields the area; the area of a right triangle equals one half the base multiplied by the height. Again, total all areas and add 10 percent for waste and extras. Do not subtract for chimneys, air vents, and small skylights. Then divide by 100 for the total number of squares needed.

You'll need one 36-inch x 144-foot roll of felt underlayment per three squares of shingles.

Storing Shingles

Composition shingles have adhesive blobs that, when warmed by the sun, seal each tab. For this reason, shingles must be stacked out of the sun. Bundles also must be protected from the rain. Shingles are best stored on a skid and covered with plastic.

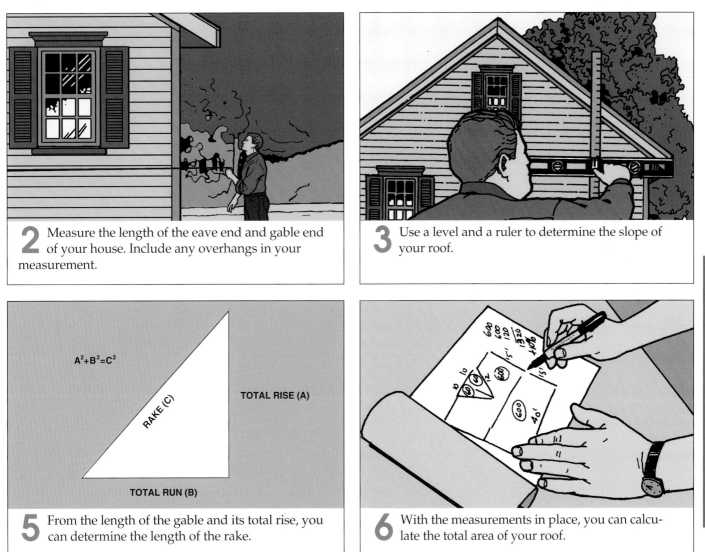

2 Measure the length of the eave end and gable end of your house. Include any overhangs in your measurement.

3 Use a level and a ruler to determine the slope of your roof.

$A^2+B^2=C^2$

TOTAL RISE (A)

RAKE (C)

TOTAL RUN (B)

5 From the length of the gable and its total rise, you can determine the length of the rake.

6 With the measurements in place, you can calculate the total area of your roof.

3 Asphalt Shingles

The most physically demanding part of roofing is getting the shingles on the roof. Many suppliers offer this service, which is well worth the additional expense (right).

If the job is going to be spread over several evenings and weekends, carry up only as many shingles that can be applied in a day. Partial bundles can be carried across one's padded head, or whole bundles can be supported on one padded shoulder (center and center right). Most shingle bundles weigh about 75 pounds.

If you would rather not carry the shingles up by hand, use a ladderveyor (below). Be sure to read the ladder safety tips found on pages 9–10.

A bundle set on either side of the ridge forms a level base for stacking additional bundles. Doing this provides an open work area (below right).

Starting a New Roof or Tear-Off

Apply a starter course directly on top of the roofing felt or ice guard. Cut the tabs off of full shingles. Trim 3 inches off one side of the first shingle so that joints are staggered rather than lined up with the first course of shingles. Staggering joints prevents leaks. Apply the starter course so that it is flush with the drip edge. (The asphalt strips will be 1 inch above the drip edge.) If there is no drip edge, allow the starter strip to overhang the edge of the eaves by ¼ to ⅜ inch. Be sure any nails will be covered by shingles above.

Ice Guard. Local building codes may require that you install a roll roofing ice guard to prevent leaks from ice dams. There are no joints, so you do not have to worry about staggering. Some products are self-adhesive, so you don't have to nail it; others are "self-sealing."

Applying Rake Edge. If the rake edge (the roof edge above the gable) is badly deteriorated, install a border of whole shingles along the rake edge. Keep the upper edge of the shingle toward the rake edge with tabs inward. Allow ¼- to ⅜-inch overhang. Nail every 10 to 12 inches, 3 to 4 inches in from the edge.

When you are starting a new roof or reroofing after tearing off the old roof, first install a drip edge along the eave-edge of the roof; then cover the roof sheathing with roofing felt.

Many professional roofers snap vertical chalk lines from the eaves to the ridge and horizontal lines across the roof to help keep three-tab shingles aligned. You can snap vertical lines at 30 and 36 inches for 6-inch exposure and 24 and 36 inches for 4-inch exposure, and in mutiples of 36 inches thereafter if you'd like. Snap horizontal lines every fourth course or so going up the roof.

Before applying full shingles, attach a starter course to the edge of the roof. The starter course places the adhesive strip about 1 inch up from the edge of the roof. The tabs on the first full course will adhere to this strip. Align the first course to the edge, and then snap a chalk line for the second course. Stagger the joints on the shingles, and follow the nailing pattern established by the shingle manufacturer.

1. Staple builder's felt to the roof. Cut the strips to span the full width of the roof. Align the first strip with the bottom edge of the roof, and staple it down. The second course should overlap the first by 4 to 6 in.

2. Install drip edge to protect the edges of the sheathing. Along the lower edge of the roof, the roofing felt overlaps the drip edge. Along the gable edges, install the drip edge overlapping the felt.

3. Snap vertical guidelines (here, 30 and 36 inches from the edge of the planned overhang). Cut the tabs off some shingles, and begin shingling with the starter course.

4. Lay the first full course of shingles with the tabs overlaying the starter course. Follow the nailing pattern specified by the manufacturer on the packaging. Typically, you use four nails per shingle, positioning them above the notch between tabs.

3 Asphalt Shingles

Working with a Reroof

Adding Drip Edge. If shingles at the edge of the eaves are deteriorated cut them back flush with the fascia or old drip edge below. Add a metal drip edge to prevent moisture from getting under the shingles. This protects the fascia boards from rot and provides a finished appearance and a straight, strong edge. Apply the drip edge using roofing nails.

Applying Reroof Starter. When reroofing, the starter strip is just wide enough to cover the exposure of the first course of old shingles. Make a starter strip by cutting the tabs off of several shingles. The resulting strip is 4 to 5 inches wide.

Trim 3 inches off one side of the first strip so that no joints between strips fall over joints between old roofing shingles. Nail it in place with four nails at 3 or 4 inches above the eaves edge. If you added a drip edge, bring the edge of the starter course even with the edge of the drip edge. If you did not use a drip edge, allow the starter strip to extend ¼ to ⅜ inch beyond the edge of the eaves.

Adding Drip Edge. If the edges of existing shingles are deteriorated, cut them back and add a drip edge.

Applying Reroof Starter. Cut the tabs off shingles for starter strips. Trim 3 in. to stagger the joints.

Tips for Cutting Shingles

■ Hook blades specially made for cutting roofing fit in a standard utility knife.

■ Some roofers prefer straight blades because you can use them to "gang-cut" through several shingles at the same time. Gang-cutting is handy when you are cutting lots of tabs for a ridge or hip. Granules quickly dull the blades of utility knives, so be sure to have plenty of extras on hand. Shingles tear when cut with a dull blade.

■ In cool weather, it is faster to cut shingles from the side that is not granulated.

■ When a neat, straight cut is required (as when cutting off a tab at the end of a course), a metal square can be used as a straightedge to guide the blade.

Nailing Shingles Properly

Shingles are typically attached with four nails; one at each end and one above each tab slot. In windy areas some roofers use six nails, adding one to either side of each tab slot. Note that nails are positioned just beneath the adhesive, but above the tops of the slots. Nails also must be long enough to penetrate the sheathing by ¾ inch. This rule applies whether fastening the shingles to a new roof or to a reroof.

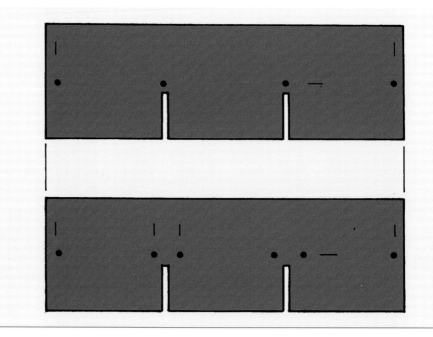

Basic Shingling

Nothing is more frustrating than hammering four to six nails into a shingle only to find that it is crooked. The procedure below will help you get the shingle aligned right the first time.

1 Lining Up the Shingle. Begin by aligning the upper corner of the shingle with the upper corner of the shingle already in place. Tack a nail to hold it in place.

2 Tacking Opposite End. Position the opposite end of the shingle. (Some people do this by simply eyeballing where the tab hits the shingle on the previous course. Others use the gauge built into a roofing hammer.) Tack in place.

3 Checking and Nailing. Give the shingle a quick double-check for alignment. Then, beginning from the left (if you are right-handed) nail the first tacked nail home and work across the course, carefully flattening out bulges. If necessary, remove one of the tacked nails to eliminate buckling.

Tips for Fastening

Whether you choose to hammer nails or apply staples driven by a pneumatic gun, the following tips help to achieve a secure fastening job:

■ Use zinc-coated nails to prevent corrosion.

■ Avoid exposing fasteners. Each row of shingles must cover the fasteners of the previous course.

■ Do not drive the fastener so deep that its head breaks the surface of the shingle.

■ A nail that penetrates too easily may work its way out. Remove it and seal the hole.

■ Always drive fasteners in straight so that the heads lay flat. Nailheads that stick up at an angle can wear through the shingle above.

■ Do not nail into or above an adhesive strip.

■ If using staples, make sure they are set properly. (See below.)

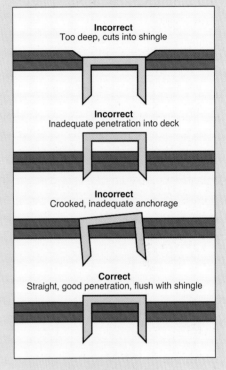

Incorrect
Too deep, cuts into shingle

Incorrect
Inadequate penetration into deck

Incorrect
Crooked, inadequate anchorage

Correct
Straight, good penetration, flush with shingle

1 Align the upper corner of the new shingle with the upper corner of the adjacent shingle.

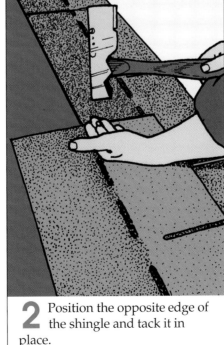

2 Position the opposite edge of the shingle and tack it in place.

3 Drive in the tacked nails across the shingle.

3 Asphalt Shingles

Choosing a Shingle Pattern

Before you put your nailing skills to work, you must choose a shingle pattern. Each pattern requires standard three-tab shingles, which are positioned differently to achieve different effects. Each offsets the tab cutouts of overlapping courses by a different distance.

Six-Inch Method. The most common method of aligning shingles is called the 6-inch method. Each course starts at a 6-inch offset to the course below. This is handy because it neatly cuts tabs in half and therefore minimizes waste. The result is a neat arrangement where each tab lines up with the tab two courses above or below.

Four- and Five-Inch Methods. Though the 6-inch method is the easiest to cut and apply, some builders are concerned with the way every other vertical cutout lines up and as a result creates a flow path that may erode shingles. This issue is still being debated, but there are other patterns that avoid the problem altogether. The 4-inch method is diagonal in appearance, with two full shingles between tab slots. The 5-inch method provides a bit more offset and more of a diagonal pattern to the shingles.

Random Shingling. With random shingling, each course is offset a multiple of 3 inches. The order of the multiples—whether they be 3, 6, 9, or 12 inches of offset—varies. The effect is a look with no discernible pattern and with some of the character of random-width wooden shingles or slates.

Six-Inch Method. The 6-in. method is the easiest and most common shingling pattern. Alternating tab cutouts are aligned.

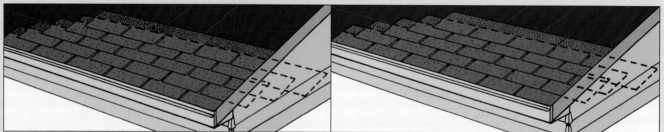

Four- and Five-Inch Method. With the 4-in. method, tab cutouts align vertically only every fourth course (left) instead of every other course. A pleasing diagonal effect results when shingles are trimmed in 5 in. increments (right), and tab cuouts never exactly align.

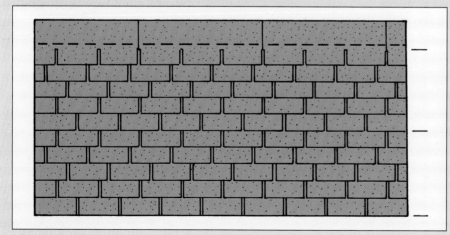

Random Shingling. This random pattern uses 3-in. cutouts in a varied order to achieve a look similar to wood shingles or slate. Tab cutouts occasionally align, but not in a regular pattern.

Choosing to Hammer

Professional roofers who nail by hand are a vanishing breed. As a do-it-yourselfer you have two options. If you are able to set aside a block of time to complete the roof in one go, you can rent a pneumatic stapler. (Ask the rental dealer to demonstrate safe use of the equipment.) However, renting equipment results in added expenses and the additional time it takes to learn how to use that equipment. Breaking out a simple hammer is often the better choice. The following is a professional nailing technique that speeds a hammering job along.

Holding a Handful. Hold a dozen or so nails loosely in your hand. Using only one hand, work a nail around so it hangs head up between your fingers (left).

Hammering the Nail Home. Position the nail on the shingle using the nail hand only (center). Nail it.

Working Nails into Position. While one hand is nailing, the other hand is busy readying the next nail (right).

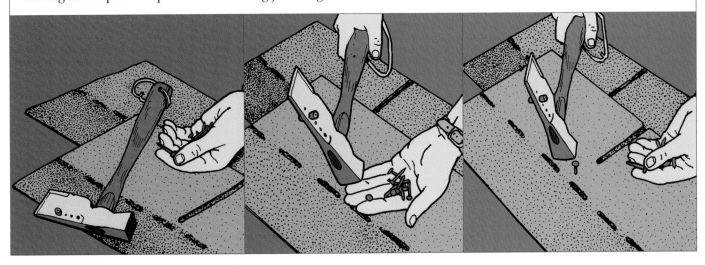

Using a Roofing Hammer

A roofing hammer speeds up any roofing job, and although it is a relatively expensive tool, it is worth the investment if you are doing a large roofing job. A roofing hammer's heavy weight is an advantage for quickly whacking nails home, but be careful of its serrated head, which is especially hard on fingers if you miss the nail.

With a built-in course gauge set according to the exposure desired, this hammer is far more precise and much faster than simply eyeballing the top of the shingles. The guide pin can be set in any one of the several holes for the desired course depth (left).

Hook the pin on the course below, and let the bottom edge of the shingle rest against the heel of the hammer (center).

The hatchet side of the hammer is designed for splitting wood shingles to size (right). It is less useful for composition shingles, but it's still good for chopping out old roofing cement or flashing.

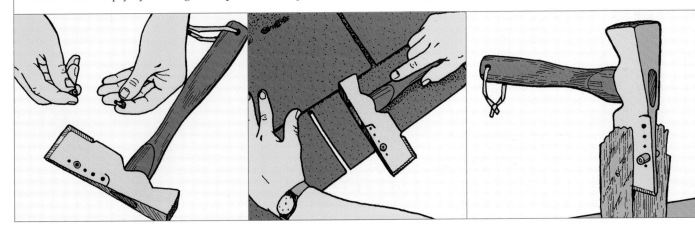

Shingling a Stair-Step Pattern

At this point the roof is prepared for shingling, the shingles are ordered, and the shingling pattern has been chosen. The following is a step-by-step approach to the 6-inch pattern. Except when it comes to the amount of shingle that must be trimmed, the same instructions apply to the other shingling patterns.

Rather than working across the roof one row at a time (and moving ladders, cleats, etc. each time) experienced roofers stair-step as many courses as they can safely reach—and as far across as roof brackets permit. By building up a stair-step pattern of shingles along the left-hand eaves of the roof (left-handed shinglers work from the right side of the roof), you can add on a series of whole shingles without moving the roof cleats.

1 Precutting Shingles. Set up a work area on the ground. A 4 x 4-foot scrap of plywood on a sawhorse is ideal. Using an angle square and a utility knife equipped with a roofing hook blade, cut a series of partial shingles so you can stair-step up five courses. (Save scrap pieces for possible use as filler at the opposite end of the roof.)

2 Starting the Course. The first shingles are placed over the eaves course (the first course of shingles laid as the starter course). Double-check to be sure seams between shingles do not line up with seams in the starter course.

3 Building the Stair-Step. Remove one half of a tab from a shingle and use this shingle to begin the second course. If you are using a roofing hammer, use the gauge to keep course depth consistent. Continue adding partial shingles along the rake to achieve the stair-step pattern. Once the pattern is complete you can add course after course of whole shingles.

4 Checking and Aligning. Almost all composition shingles have alignment notches in the middle of each tab along the upper edge of the shingle. These are especially useful when beginning courses. Pinch one side of the alignment notch upright so the new shingle butts against it. Roofs are seldom perfectly square, so it's a good idea to strike horizontal (every four courses) and vertical (as needed) chalk lines as guides for the subsequent courses.

Nesting

When applying new shingles directly over the old, the roof first must be brushed to remove any debris or loose granules. New shingles are then "nested" over the old shingles. This maintains the old exposure and provides a quick way to align the new shingles because you push the tops of the new shingles against the bottom tabs of the old. The result is a smooth, uniform covering.

Nesting is simple. Begin by trimming the tabs off a whole shingle to make a starter strip. It fits just between the eaves edge and the bottom of the second course of shingles. Note that the tab adhesive provides a good seal at the eaves. In positioning the starter strip, be sure to adequately overlap tab cutouts on the first course of the old roof. Once the starter strip is in place, proceed with the courses, positioning them so that cutouts offset the old cutouts by 3 inches.

Nesting. The nesting method of applying new shingles over old provides even coverage and quick course alignment.

1 A stair-step pattern starts each course with a shingle half a tab less than the course above.

2 To ensure that the cutouts align vertically, follow guidelines and use the shingle alignment notches.

3 Stair-step the pieces in place along the rake edge.

4 Measure every four courses or so to check that courses are running parallel with the eaves.

Vertical Guides at 36" and 30" from Rake End

Vertical Guide

Ribbon Courses

A ribbon course adds interest to the standard 6-inch pattern.

After six courses have been applied, cut a 4-inch-wide strip lengthwise off the upper section of a shingle. Nail it as the seventh course ¼ inch below the top of the cutouts of the sixth course. Then reverse the 8-inch-wide leftover scrap and nail it on top of the 4-inch strip (left). Cover both with the next full course. Doing this creates a three-ply edge also known as the ribbon (right).

Working on Steep Slopes

It is extremely difficult to work on a high-pitched roof. A scaffold is a necessity in these situations. Unless you own a scaffold and are experienced in using it, it's best to hire a contractor to handle steep roofs.

Roofs that exceed a slope of 21 in 12 (a mansard roof is likely to have this sort of slope) render factory-applied, self-sealing adhesive ineffective. This is because the extreme pitch makes it impossible for heat and gravity to complete the seal. In this case use extra sealant. Put a quarter-size dab of quick-setting roofing cement under each tab as you shingle. Also, apply six fasteners to each shingle: one at each end and two above and to each side of each tab cutout.

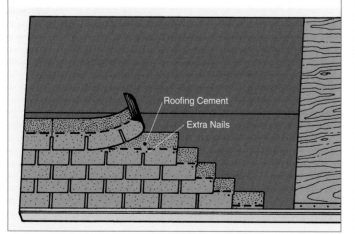

Working on Low Slopes

Water tends to be blown under shingles applied to low slopes, so special precautions must be taken. Where the rise is 2 to 4 inches in 12, use square-tab shingles with double underlayment and roofing cement. (A roof with a slope of less than 2 in 12 cannot be covered with tab shingles. Use roll or built-up roofing instead.) Apply a double thickness of underlayment, lapping each course over the preceding one by 19 inches. Start with a 19-inch strip at the eaves. If you live in a cold climate, protect against ice dams by cementing together the two felt layers up to a point 2 feet inside the interior wall line of the house.

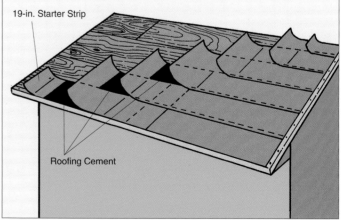

Roofing the Valleys

Valleys are among the most difficult and most important areas to roof. A valley forms the junction between two planes on a roof and must carry off a great deal of water. The two types of valleys are called open and closed. Open valleys create a channel down which water flows. Closed valleys are shingled over completely. The valley is the most vulnerable section of a roof. During a torrent, water is sometimes driven under shingles on either side of the valley, causing leaks. Always avoid stepping in a valley when working on the roof.

Building Open Valleys

1 Applying Roll Roofing. Fill in the valley with an 18-inch piece of roll roofing. Roll out the length needed from a 36 inch-wide roll. Then flip it over; strike a line at 18 inches; and cut with a utility knife. Roll it up again before carrying it up to the roof.

Coat the valley with roofing cement, and lay the piece of roll roofing granule-face down. Drive a nail every 12 inches down one side. Nail the other side after nesting the piece completely into the valley, leaving no voids beneath. Then center a full-width (36-inch) piece over it, granules up. Nail along one edge only. Let the roofing run wide, which means you just let extra lengths of roofing flop over the ridge and eaves to be trimmed later. Split the roofing at the ridge and eaves so it lays flat. Trim the lower edge flush with the eaves, and cut a slight radius at the inside corner on the intersection of the eaves.

2 Shingling and Trimming. Use a chalk line to mark the center of the valley. Continue installing shingles until they reach the valley. Make sure the last shingle in each course ends within 3 inches of the centerline. Then strike guidelines for trimming the shingles. Start the lines 6 inches apart at top and let them diverge ⅛ inch per foot toward the eaves.

3 Nipping Corners. Slip a scrap of roofing under the shingles, and trim the new shingles using a utility knife with a hook blade. Be careful not to pierce the roll roofing. When one side is completely trimmed, work your way back up the other side, trimming the uppermost corner of each shingle. This prevents the corner from catching water and pulling it under the shingle.

4 Nailing and Cementing Shingles. Nail the shingles at least 4 inches from the trim edge. Use roofing cement to seal down the shingles.

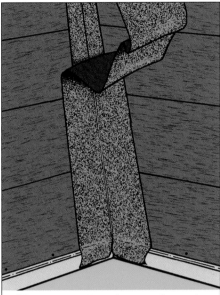

1 Open valleys have a channel of doubled roll roofing, the first layer laid granule face down.

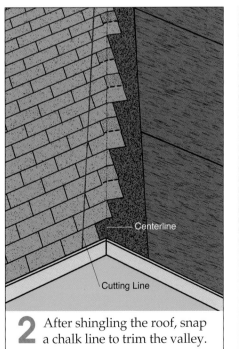

Centerline

Cutting Line

2 After shingling the roof, snap a chalk line to trim the valley.

3 Use a utility knife to trim the uppermost corner off each shingle along the valley.

4 Cement shingles to each other and to the roll roofing in the valley.

Building Closed Valleys

Closed valleys have no channel and are created by continuing the roofing material across the valley. A woven valley (sometimes referred to as a laced valley) is the quickest type of closed valley to install. A slightly more time-consuming variation is the half-weave valley (sometimes called closed-cut or half-laced valley), in which the overlapping layer of roofing is neatly trimmed.

Both types begin with one layer of 36-inch-wide roll roofing. Hold the roll roofing in place with temporary nails tapped lightly into the surface 1 inch from the outer edge of the valley. (The nails from the shingles fasten it permanently later.) Be careful to work roofing into the valley cavity. This job is easier done on a warm day, as warm shingles become pliable enough to lay down completely and without voids. Trim excess at eaves. At the ridge, allow the piece to flop over the opposite roof face.

Full Weave. Complete shingling adjacent planes of the roof that meet at the valley. With a helper, complete the shingling of each plane, weaving the shingles by laying alternate shingles down at each course and pushing them into the valley. Clip the uppermost corner of every overlapping shingle. Apply two nails at the side of the shingle that crosses the valley.

Do not nail within 6 inches of the centerline of a valley. If the pitch of the roof differs on either side of the valley you may have to weave as many as three shingles on one side to one on the other.

Building Closed Valleys. A woven valley is made up of interlacing shingles from adjacent roof faces. The job is done quickly but does not offer the best protection or appearance.

Half-Weave. The half-weave valley is a variation on the woven valley. Begin by laying down roll roofing as described. Completely shingle one side of the roof, overlapping the valley at least 12 inches beyond the centerline. Next, shingle the opposite side, letting the shingles overlap the finished side. Clip the uppermost corner of every overlapping shingle. Do not nail within 6 inches of the centerline of the valley. Strike a chalkline down the center of the valley, and trim the shingles. Trim corners nearest the valley, and seal shingles with roofing cement.

Full Weave. In this case, overlaps stack up on one side to compensate for the difference in pitch. Do not nail within 6 in. of the centerline of a valley.

Half Weave. One group of shingles is laid across the valley. Shingles on the opposite side are trimmed to bisect the valley with a crisp line.

As the valley leads you up one side of the dormer, you probably are wondering how to evenly match the courses of shingles on the other side. Once you have worked your way to a dormer and have completed one valley, continue the topmost course past the ridge of the dormer. Chalk a line that extends the course. If possible, check the trueness of the extended line by measuring down from the roof ridge. Nail along the top of the course only so that shingles may be slipped under it later.

Once the course is extended about 10 feet, strike parallel chalk lines 36 inches apart to serve as a guide for aligning cutouts as the other side of the dormer is shingled. As you complete shingling on the other side of the dormer, check course alignment as well. Fortunately, shingles are a forgiving material and slight adjustments, if made over several courses or shingles, are not noticeable.

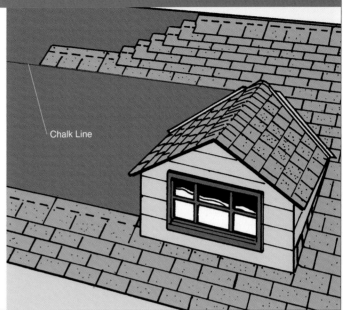

Chalk Line

Air Vents and Plumbing Stacks

Shingling around Air Vents. Reroofing (or tearing off and adding a new roof) presents the opportunity to add new air vents to the attic. Old, dented vents also can be replaced while you are on the roof. The roofing principles for handling air vents and plumbing stacks are the same: flashing covers shingles below the object; shingles overlap the flashing above the object. Adhere the vent with a coating of roofing cement.

Shingling around Stacks. The most thorough way to roof around a stack is to remove the flashing. Older homes have lead flashing while newer homes have aluminum or vinyl flashing or a rubber boot and flashing. (Replacement stack flashing can be readily purchased if the old flashing is damaged.) Continue the courses of roofing beneath the vent, notching them with a utility knife to fit around the pipe. Nail and cement the flashing into place so that it covers the courses below. Continue the courses so that those halfway above the pipe overlap the flashing. Notch them as necessary, and seal them with roofing cement.

The flashing around a plumbing stack overlaps the same shingles that the stack pierces. Trim an overlapping tab so that it surrounds the stack. Use roofing cement to seal the job.

Shingling around Air Vents. Install air vents so that shingles cover at least the top half of the vent flashing. Work roofing cement under the flashing. Nail the bottom edges with galvanized roofing nails, and cover the heads with roofing cement.

Shingling around Stacks. Fit the vent collar onto the stack and over the new roofing. Fasten it with roofing cement. Shingles should overlap only the upper half of the vent collar. Trim the overlapping shingles around the stack, maintaining a ½-in. gap. Seal the shingle tabs down with roofing cement.

3 Asphalt Shingles

Shingling Ridges

The ridge of your roof runs from the peak of one gable to the peak of the other. Here's how to shingle the ridge using shingles if your roof doesn't have a ridge vent. (For information on ridge vents, see page 78.)

1 Gang-Cutting Tabs. Ridges are made by cutting single tabs off of shingles. The easiest way to do this is to stack a bunch of shingles neatly together. Use a square as a guide as you cut through the first shingle to separate the tabs. Taper the cuts slightly as shown in the drawing. Then you can use the top shingle as a guide to slice through the shingles below.

2 Trimming Final Course. Wrap ridge shingle piece over the ridge to check whether you need another course of shingles on either slope. Trim the last course of shingles to fit just up to the ridge.

3 Wrapping the Ridge. Strike a chalk line on the most visible side of the house, usually the front. Wrap a single tab over the ridge, making sure the alignment notch centers the very apex. Use this as a guide for snapping the line. If there is a prevailing wind direction in your area, work toward it. Apply one nail at either side of each tab and just in front of the sealant line.

4 Topping it Off. Nail the final shingle, and cover the nailheads with roofing cement. Seal each tab with roofing cement for a truly windproof ridge.

5 Mitering Ridge Shingles. Begin the ridge of a hip roof with a single tab mitered to suit the shape of the eaves. Position the tab; mark along the eaves line at either side; and cut using a square as a guide. Work along the ridge in the same way you would for a gable ridge. At the top of the hip ridge, miter adjacent tabs and overlap them with a tab that has been specially cut and folded into a cap.

Finishing Up

A caulk gun loaded with a tube of roofing cement is a handy tool when it comes to finishing up the job. It can be used to seal tabs where roof cleats were suspended, to seal nails on gutter hangers, to coat bolts that hold antennas to the roof, and to seal tabs that may have curled at the edges (below).

Strike a chalk line where the shingles overlap the rake. Then use a utility knife to trim the rake edges (right).

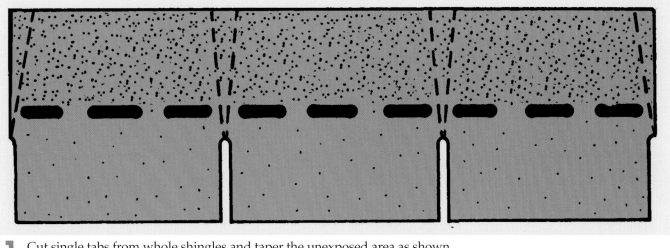

1 Cut single tabs from whole shingles and taper the unexposed area as shown.

2 Apply and trim the final course of shingles. Trim the last course of shingles on each slope to end at the ridge.

3 Strike a chalk line, and apply the shingles with a 5-in. exposure.

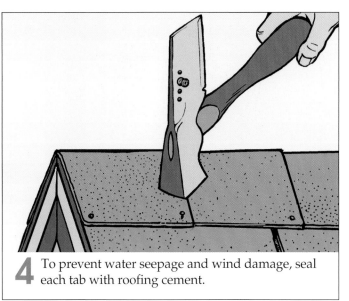

4 To prevent water seepage and wind damage, seal each tab with roofing cement.

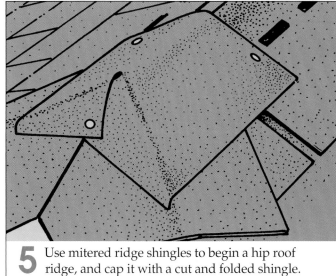

5 Use mitered ridge shingles to begin a hip roof ridge, and cap it with a cut and folded shingle.

wood shingles

Roofing with Wood

Wood shingles and shakes usually are made of Western red cedar, a long-lasting, straight-grained wood. The grain is what gives the wood surprising strength whether it is cut thick or very thin. Even after years of weathering, wood does a much better job of shedding water than might be expected. In addition, wood shingles and shakes resist heat transmission twice as well as composition shingles.

Wood shingles often require more maintenance than other roofing options, especially if you live in a harsh climate. In such areas it is advisable to treat wood shingles and shakes with a preservative every five years or so. Regular cleaning also is recommended to clear away debris that traps moisture and breeds fungus, mildew, rot, and insect borers. Wood shingles and shakes are not fire resistant and some local codes may even require that the wood be pressure treated. Some localities have banned wood roofing altogether; be sure to check your local codes before deciding to use wood shingles or shakes. In addition, check with your insurance company to see if your premiums will be affected.

Choosing Between Shingles and Shakes

Shingles are thinner than shakes and are sawn smooth on both sides. Shakes often are split by hand rather than cut and have a very irregular surface. They are thicker and therefore more durable than shingles, which typically last no more than 20 to 25 years. There are two common types of shakes used in residential roofing. One type, called tapersplit, is split on both sides. Tapersplits are made by hand. The other type, called handsplit and resawn, is split from the block and then sawn to produce two shingles, each with one split and one sawn face.

Straight-split shakes do not taper in thickness (as do all other wood shingles and shakes) and are not intended for residential use.

Both shakes and shingles are available in number 1, 2, and 3 grades. Grade number 1 is cut from heartwood, a clear (knot-free), completely edge-grained wood that is the more resistant to rot than the other grades. It is also the most expensive of the grades. Buy the best grade you can afford. Grade number 2 has a limited amount of sapwood. (Sapwood is less rot-resistant than heartwood.) In addition, number 2 grade has some knots and is flat grained. It is acceptable for residential roofing. Use grade number 3 shingles or shakes for outbuildings only. Shingles also come in a grade 4, which has large knots and is only acceptable for a starter course. Shakes don't come in grade 4.

The shingle length needed is determined by the desired exposure (the length of shingle exposed to weather). Exposure is determined by pitch. Shingle widths vary from 3 to 9 inches.

Reroofing with Shingles and Shakes

With the proper preparation you can shingle over a roof of wood shingles. However, you cannot shingle over shakes due to their irregular shape. Both shingles and shakes can be installed over composition shingles.

In order to install shingles and shakes, the roof must have a large enough slope. The reason for this is simple. Unlike self-sealing composition shingles or roll roofing, voids remain between courses of wood shingles and shakes. With enough pitch for quick runoff this poses no problem, but when installed on a low-slope, roof shingles are not protected from windblown rain and snow.

Shingles are not recommended for roofs with less than a 3-in-12 slope. (See "Estimating Materials for Gabled Roofs," pages 32–33.) Shakes are not recommended for roofs with a slope of less than a 4 in 12. Exposure also must be limited for slight slopes. For example, with a 3-in-12 slope, 16-inch shingles must have a maximum of 3¾-inch exposure (5 inches on a 4-in-12 slope). Eighteen-inch shingles may be exposed a maximum of 4¼ inches (5½ inches on a 4-in-12 slope). Shingles that are 24 inches long can have the greatest exposure (5¾ inches on a 3-in-12 slope and 7½ inches on a 4-in-12 slope).

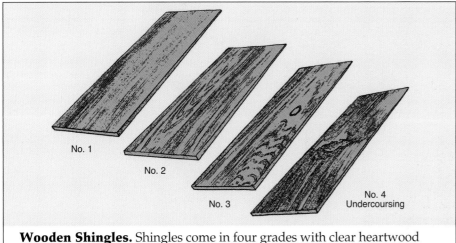

Wooden Shingles. Shingles come in four grades with clear heartwood being the best and undercoursing being the worst.

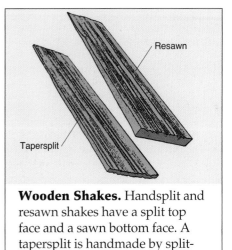

Wooden Shakes. Handsplit and resawn shakes have a split top face and a sawn bottom face. A tapersplit is handmade by splitting on both sides.

Nailing Patterns

Apply shingles and shakes with only two nails per shingle. As the courses overlap, four nails pierce each shingle or shake. Place nails about ¾ inch from each edge and 1 to 2 inches above the lowest edge of the overlapping course. Stagger joints at least 1½ inches.

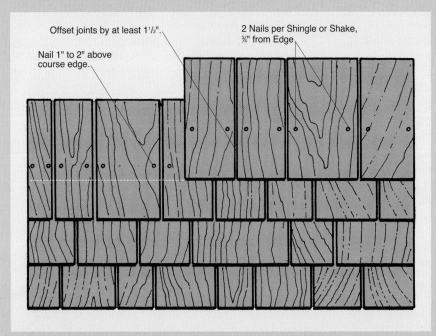

Nailing Patterns. Each shingle or shake is applied with two nails. Due to overlapping courses, four nails ultimately hold each shingle.

Nailing Guides

To keep courses straight, tack a 1x4 guide in place for each course or use the adjustable gauge on a roofing hammer.

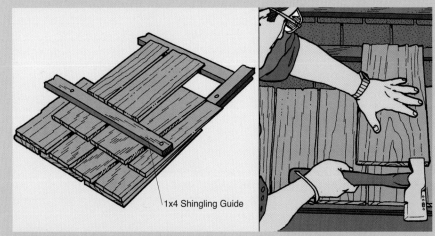

Nailing Guides. For quick application and a crisp finish use a guide board for positioning shingles or shakes (left). A roofing hammer with an adjustable course guide speeds up the job of aligning shingles (right).

Building Special Helpers

Wood shingles and shakes are slippery compared to the gritty grab of composition shingles, so it's a good idea to use a toeboard to help keep yourself and your materials on the roof. A toeboard is simply a long 2x4. Use three shakes or shingles as shown to shim the toeboard off the roof, giving you a deeper toe hold. Use 16d or 20d nails through the toeboard, shims, roofing and sheathing and into the rafter below. For a handy place to nest a bundle of shingles, nail two scrap shingles upright on the toeboards. Use a toeboard every 3 or 4 feet up the roof.

A simple seat with a spiked base that grips the newly applied shingles also comes in handy. Build it with plywood and 1x4s. Drill ¹⁄₁₆-inch pilot holes and screw the pieces together with 6 x 1⅝ galvanized deck screws. Drive roofing nails through the 1x4s before attaching them to the seat. The nails stick into the roof to keep you from sliding.

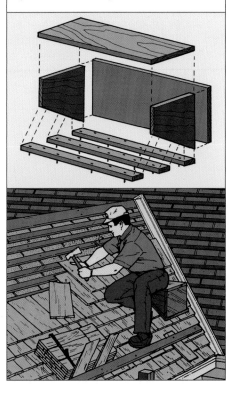

Applying Sheathing and Underlayment

Wood roofing benefits greatly from ventilation so it almost always has spaced sheathing. The space allows shingles to dry after rain thereby preventing rot. Solid sheathing, however, still is used at ridges, eaves, rakes, and places exposed to great amounts of wind and snow.

Always use 30-pound felt underlayment when installing shakes. The irregular shape of the shakes allows plenty of air circulation. For wood shingles use underlayment only in areas where ice may collect and at the eaves and rakes.

Before laying shakes (not shingles) nail a drip edge along the eaves. Begin by laying a full sheet of felt. All subsequent sheets are 18 inches wide. If you cannot purchase 18-inch felt, cut the sheets to size.

When adding a layer of new shingles over old, ventilation channels are made by installing a new underlayment. This process includes removing old shingles, furring out the ridge, renewing the valley flashing, and adding a 1x6 nailer at the eaves and rakes.

By adding a similar system of underlayment, wood shingles can be installed on top of composition shingles. Trim back the composition shingles where they extend beyond the edge of the roof before installing underlayment.

Covering Wood Shingles

1 **Removing the Ridge.** Use a flat shovel or crowbar to remove the old ridge.

2 **Renewing the Valley.** Fur out the valley to bring it to the level of the original shingles. Resurface with new flashing.

3 **Reinforcing the Ridge.** Beveled siding turned upside down reinforces the ridge and counteracts the bevel of the last course of shingles.

4 **Sheathing Rake and Eaves.** Use the sharp edge of a roofing hammer to cut away shingles along the rake and eaves. Open a cavity into which a 1x6 piece of sheathing can be nailed.

1 The first step in adding a new layer to an old wood roof is to pry off the old ridge with a crowbar or a flat shovel.

2 Use 1x3s to fill in the valleys so they will be flush with the old roof. Resurface by installing W-metal flashing.

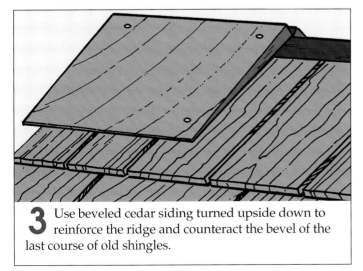

3 Use beveled cedar siding turned upside down to reinforce the ridge and counteract the bevel of the last course of old shingles.

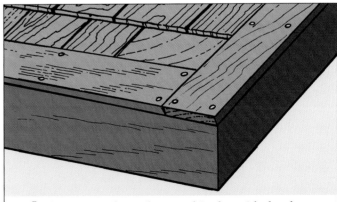

4 Cut away rake and eaves shingles with the sharp edge of a roofing hammer to make room for 1x6 sheathing.

Covering Asphalt Shingles

1 **Trimming Back.** Use a sharpened roofing hammer to cut away the overhang created by the old composition shingles.

2 **Applying Solid Sheathing.** Using 8d galvanized nails, add 1x6 sheathing to provide a solid nailing surface at the ridge, rakes, and eaves. Use pairs of 1x3s in the valleys.

3 **Applying Ventilation Strips.** Space 1x3s a distance equal to the desired exposure of the shingles. Metal flashing is applied to the valley before installing shingle courses. (See "Renewing the Valley," page 51.)

1 Trim the old shingles flush to the rake with a utility knife or sharp roofing hammer.

2 Sheathe ridge, rakes, eaves, and valley with 1x6 boards fastened with 8d galvanized nails.

3 Ventilation strips, sometimes called "skip" sheathing, allow air to pass between the shingles and the asphalt roof. The strips are made of 1x3s.

Installing Shingles

1 Aligning First Shingles. Lay a starter course that overhangs the eaves by 1 inch. To establish a straight line tack a shingle at either end of the eaves, positioning it so it overhangs the rake by ¼ to ⅜ inch and the eaves by 1 inch.

2 Lining Up the Starter Course. Tack a nail into the butt of each starter shingle at the end of the eaves, and run a line between the two. Use the line as a guide for laying the starter course.

3 Adding Courses. Leave ⅛- to ¼-inch spaces between shingles. Always stagger spaces at least 1½ inches as courses overlap. Snap a chalk line to ensure a straight second course. Set your roofing hammer (if you have one) to the correct exposure, and use it as a guide for placing the shingles. Snap a chalk line to check alignment every three or four courses. Use 3d nails for 16- and 18-inch shingles, and 4d for 24-inch shingles. Always use galvanized nails.

4 Cutting Valley Shingles. Use a spare shingle to transfer the angle of the valley to the shingles that will be installed. Align the butt of the shingle at the eaves line; mark the angle; and cut. Once you have captured this angle, shingles can be gang cut on the ground.

5 Using a Guide for Valleys. A piece of one-by carefully placed (not nailed) in the valley provides a simple guide for aligning shingles along the valley. Allow the final course at the top of the roof to extend above the ridge line. Stretch a chalk line even with the ridge line, and snap it on the shingles. Score the overhang with a utility knife. Press downward slightly to snap off the excess. Finish hips and ridges with factory-made ridge shingles.

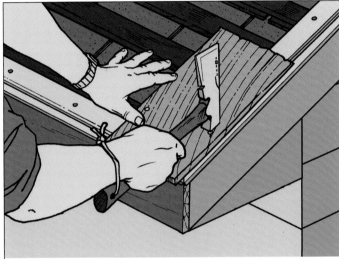

1 Install the starter course so they overhang the eaves by 1 in. and the rakes by ¼ to ⅜ in.

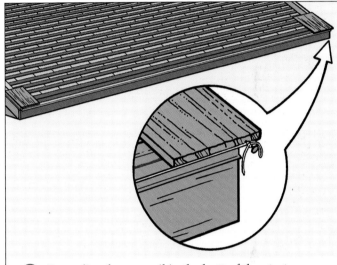

2 Run a line from a nail in the butt of the starter shingles. This line is a guide for the first course.

3 Each shingle receives two nails about ¾ in. from the edge. Use galvanized nails.

4 A spare shingle transfers the angle of the valley to the shingle to be installed.

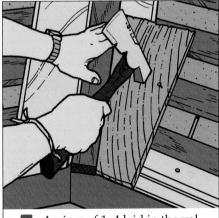

5 A piece of 1x4 laid in the valley simplifies shingle alignment. Do not nail the 1x4.

Installing Shakes

1 Applying Roll Underlayment. Unlike shingles, shakes require 18-inch underlayment sandwiched between each course. The underlayment helps shed water and blocks windblown rain. Before laying the first course, install 36-inch-wide, 15- or 30-pound felt underlayment at the eaves. (The felt weight depends on local code.) If you live in a climate with a lot of rain and snow, it is best to consider shakes only if the roof has a slope of at least 6 in 12. The irregular pattern that results with shakes provides a major advantage in that you can reroof over composition shingles or solid sheathing and allows for airflow which is crucial to wood shingles and shakes.

2 Gauging Each Course. Shakes are available in 18- and 24-inch lengths. Typical exposures are 7½ inches for 18-inch shakes and 10 inches for 24 inch shakes. You can use your hammer as an exposure guide by measuring up the handle and wrapping a piece of tape around the desired length of exposure.

Begin applying shakes with a doubled starter course that overhangs the eaves by 2 inches and the rakes by 1½ inches. To establish a straight eaves line, tack in place two shakes; one at either end of the eaves. Position each shake so it protrudes 2 inches beyond the drip edge. Hammer a nail into the edge and run a line taut between the two shakes. Each shake just touches the line as the starter course is applied. Set a similar line for the rake. Each shake receives two nails about ¾ inch from the edge. Use 7d galvanized nails for shakes.

Leave a ½-inch gap between shakes. When a course is completed, install an 18-inch-wide strip of 30-pound felt underlayment. Position the bottom edge of the felt above the shake butt at a distance equal to twice the weather exposure. Offset the gaps between shingles in neighboring courses by at least 1½ inches.

3 Marking Valley Shakes. Lay a spare shake parallel with the valley and over a shake that has been lined up even with the eaves edge. Mark a line and cut the shake. Use this shake as a template for gang-cutting shakes on a table saw.

4 Using a Guide for Valleys. A piece of one-by carefully placed (not nailed) in the valley provides a simple guide for aligning shakes that border the valley. Trim underlayment between shake courses to 2 inches short of the guide board.

5 Extending Final Courses. Allow the final courses at the top of the roof to extend above the ridge. Snap a chalk line at the ridge height, and trim shakes with a circular saw. Finish hips and ridges with factory-made ridge shakes.

1 Begin by installing 36-in.-wide underlayment along the eaves.

2 Install 18-in.-wide underlayment between courses of shakes.

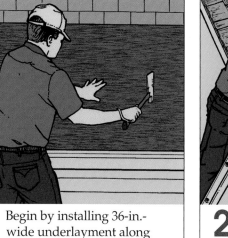

3 Use a spare shake to transfer the angle of the valley.

Trim underlayment 2 in. short of the 1x4 guide board.

4

5 Strike a line and use a circular saw to cut shakes at the ridge.

Finishing Shingles and Shakes

1 **Installing the Ridge.** Precut, factory-made ridge shingles are well worth the money. Begin by striking a line along the side of the ridge that is most visible from the ground. Use ridge shingles at either end of the ridge to set the chalk line. Alternate the mitered joint of the ridge shingles as you work up the ridge.

2 **Alternating Overlap.** If working on a peak, begin applying the ridge shingles at the end farthest from prevailing weather so that shingles overlap away from the weather. Alternate the overlap of the mitered joint of the precut ridge shingles. On the ridge of a hip roof, double the starter course at the eaves.

3 **Nailing Ridge Shingles.** Drive two nails into the midpoint of each ridge shingle and just beyond the point of overlap of the next course.

Note: When installing shakes wrap the last course of underlayment over the ridge.

4 **Installing Stack Flashing.** When applying shingles or shakes around plumbing stacks, bring the courses of shingles past the vent, and notch them with a keyhole saw or sabre saw. Cut two layers of felt slightly smaller than the base of the stack flashing. The felt fills in variations in the grain. Seal the flashing to the shingles beneath with two layers of 30-pound felt.

5 **Notching Shingles around the Stack.** Notch the next course in place. It is okay for some water to flow beneath the shingles over the flashing.

6 **Surrounding the Stack.** With wood shingles (unlike composition shingles) it is possible to completely wrap the stack without causing a back flow. To increase coverage you may choose to drop a shingle down from the final course so that it overlaps the stack flashing.

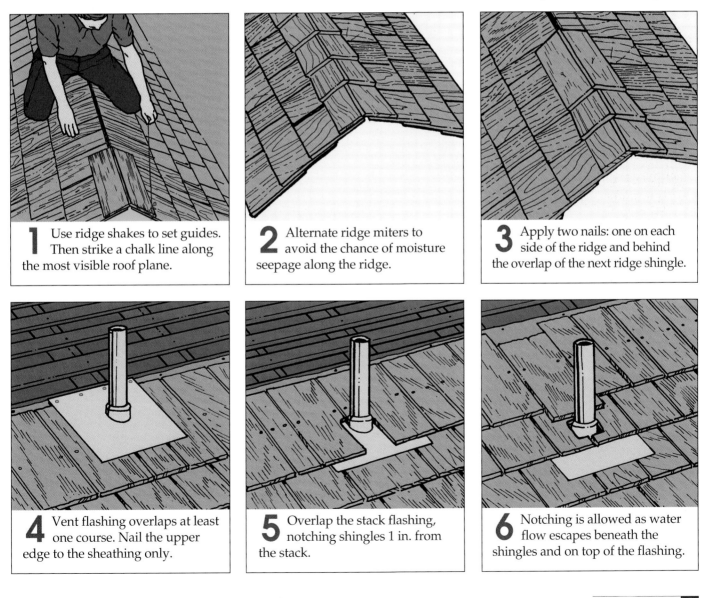

1 Use ridge shakes to set guides. Then strike a chalk line along the most visible roof plane.

2 Alternate ridge miters to avoid the chance of moisture seepage along the ridge.

3 Apply two nails: one on each side of the ridge and behind the overlap of the next ridge shingle.

4 Vent flashing overlaps at least one course. Nail the upper edge to the sheathing only.

5 Overlap the stack flashing, notching shingles 1 in. from the stack.

6 Notching is allowed as water flow escapes beneath the shingles and on top of the flashing.

Panelized Shingles

Wood shingles and shakes are available in prebonded panels, and although they are more expensive than regular shingles and shakes, they also are much quicker to install. Manufacturers claim that panels are installed twice as fast as composition shingles and four times faster than individual shakes or shingles. The panels are glued together in two- and three-ply sections that are 8 feet long. The panels are available in exposures ranging from 5½ inches (for shingles) to 9 inches (for shakes). They are applied on roofs with slopes that are 4 in 12 or greater. Each panel has a score line that is used to align courses. Install one fastener per shingle or shake (7 fasteners per panel).

1 Applying the Starter Course. If the roofing is to be applied directly over sheathing, first cover the sheathing with 15-pound felt. (Skip the felt if you are covering composition shingles.) Apply two layers of panels for the starter course, overhanging the eaves by 1½ inches and the rake by 2 inches. Nail the first layer of the starter course with two nails halfway up both ends. Then remove the felt backing from panels to be used on the second layer and nail them in place, offsetting the nails by 1½ inches. Use manufacturer-recommended fasteners. The felt backing of the panels extends 4 inches on the right of each panel, so they must be laid from left to right.

2 Applying Additional Courses. Offset subsequent courses by 6 inches. Trim 6 inches off the first panel of the second course, 12 inches off the third course, 18 inches off the third course, and so on. The seventh course panel will be about 7 inches long. The trimmings can be used on the opposite rake.

3 Trimming Valleys. Cover valleys with 36-inch felt and lay down W-metal valley flashing. (See "Valley Flasing," page 24.) Trim courses as they are applied so that they are at least 1½ inch from the centerline of the valley.

4 Roofing around Obstructions. Adjust courses as you approach a vent stack or other obstruction so you can notch the shingles without cutting into the nailing bar. Courses can be adjusted up to 2 inches per course without becoming noticeable. Make sure each course has no more than a 9-inch exposure. Adjust the courses as you approach the ridge. The goal is to end up with full-depth panels. Before installing the last course, wrap a 10-inch-wide piece of felt over the ridge. Use standard precut ridge shingles to finish the job.

1 Two layers of panels form the starter course.

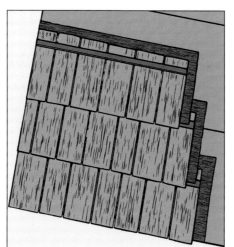

2 Work from left to right. Offset each course by 6 in.

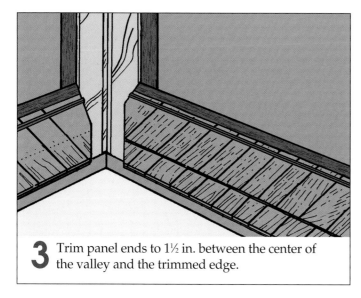

3 Trim panel ends to 1½ in. between the center of the valley and the trimmed edge.

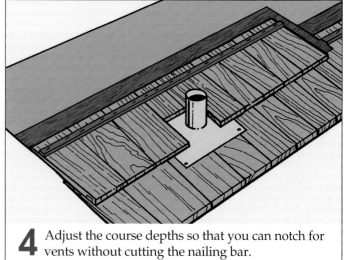

4 Adjust the course depths so that you can notch for vents without cutting the nailing bar.

Wood-Fiber Panels

Wood-fiber panels are another handy alternative to wood shingles. They are embossed with deep shadow lines and random-cut grooves that mimic the look of shakes. These 12 x 48-inch panels are applied lengthwise across the roof. They overlap with a shiplap joint between courses and a lap joint between shingles in the same course. The panels can be applied over solid sheathing or over old roofing (if the surface is sound and a layer of felt is added first). Cut the panels with a circular saw equipped with a plywood-cutting blade.

Wood-fiber panels are quick and easy to install and after a few months they weather to a silver-like gray that is very similar to cedar shingles. They can be used on roofs that have a 4-in-12 or greater slope.

1 Applying the Starter Course. Before installing wood-fiber shingles, apply a drip edge, 18-inch-wide 30-pound felt at the eaves and 36-inch-wide 30-pound felt underlayment. Cut 2½-inch-wide panel starter strips, applying them so that they overlap the eaves by 1 inch and the rakes by 2 inches. As you apply the the first course of full panels, offset the joints by 15 inches. Apply 8 fasteners per panel: begin with one centered over the shiplap joint and end with one 3 inches in from the edge.

Use 11-gauge roofing nails that penetrate ¾ inch into the deck, or 16-gauge staples that penetrate 1 inch into the deck.

2 Applying Subsequent Courses. Add the subsequent courses, offsetting end joints by at least 15 inches. The panels have two kinds of grooves in them: one type mimics the ridges found in a hand-split shake; the other type is deeper and mimics spaces between shingles. For appearance sake avoid lining up the deeper grooves even though functionally it makes no difference. Wood fiber panels have two score lines for your convenience: one for aligning the course, the other as a guide for nailing. Still, check the alignment every six or eight courses.

3 Preparing the Valleys. Line the valleys with 36-inch-wide felt and 24-inch-wide W-metal. Trim panels to within a minimum of 4 inches from the centerline of the valley, and clip 2 inches off the topmost corner of each panel along the valley.

4 Finishing Ridges and Hips. Ridges and hips are finished with manufactured caps that are scored with guidelines for spacing. After wrapping the ridge or hip with a 10-inch piece of felt, apply three fasteners in a triangular pattern to each shingle.

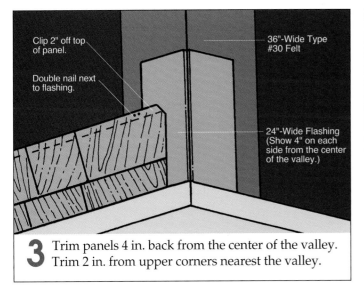

1 Cut and fasten a 2½-in. starter strip over drip edge, 18-in.-wide felt and 36-in.-wide felt.

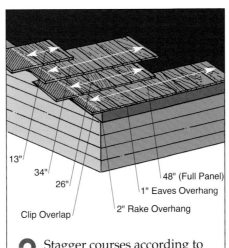

2 Stagger courses according to the pattern shown to achieve the best appearance and protection.

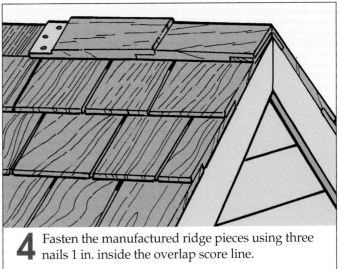

3 Trim panels 4 in. back from the center of the valley. Trim 2 in. from upper corners nearest the valley.

4 Fasten the manufactured ridge pieces using three nails 1 in. inside the overlap score line.

New Roofing

1. Wood roofing can be applied over rafters and horizontal skip sheathing.

2. Today, most wood roofing is applied over decking and a layer of roofing felt.

3. Over sheathing and felt paper, apply plastic mesh to provide air circulation.

4. Nail on drip edge along the rakes and eaves before installing the starter course.

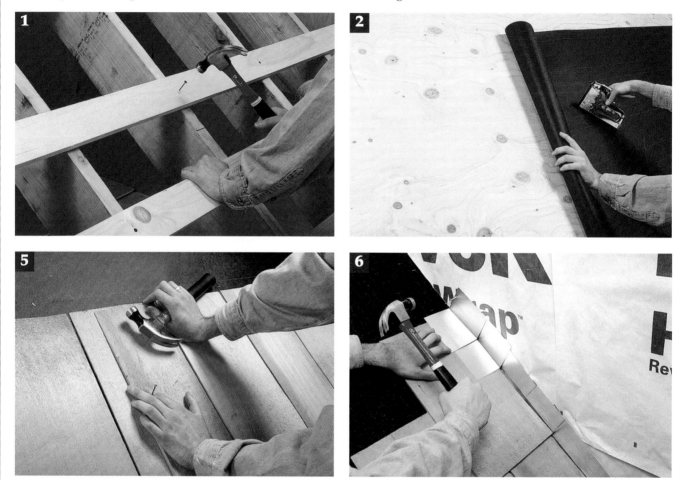

Repairing Shingles and Shakes

1. To replace damaged shingles and shakes, remove the damaged piece by first splitting it with a wood chisel.

2. Then wedge up the upper course, and cut the nails with a hacksaw blade or nail ripper.

3. Finally, after trimming the edges of a new shingle or shake to size, nail it in place, and cover exposed nailheads with roof cement.

5. The starter course should be two shingles thick and overlap eaves by 1 in.

6. When the roof butts against a second story, install step flashing at the joint.

7. Keep about ¼-in. of space between shakes by holding a pencil between them.

8. Keep the exposure consistent by using a homemade spacing jig.

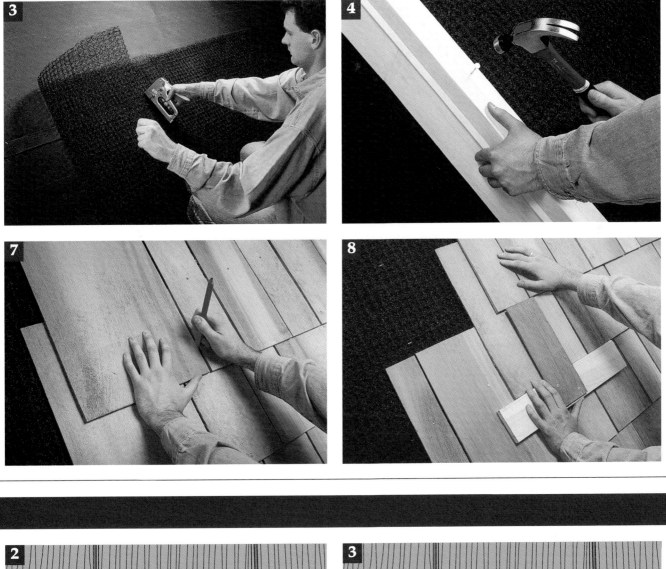

chapter 5

roll roofing

Flat Roofs

Experience has proved that an absolutely flat roof leads to trouble. To avoid standing water, which eventually causes leaks, a roof must have a minimum pitch of ¼ inch per foot. If you are reroofing on a shallower pitch, consider sheathing the roof to give it the minimal incline.

Roll roofing and built-up roofing are the most common techniques used to cover flat roofs. (Composition shingles are not used on roofs with a slope of less than 2 in 12; wood shingles are not used on a slope of less than 3 in 12; and shakes are not used on a slope of less than 4 in 12.) Of the two methods, roll roofing is quicker and easier to handle. Built-up roofing requires special equipment that cannot readily be rented. It is included in this chapter only to faciltate hiring a professional to do the job.

Roll Roofing Fundamentals

Roll roofing, which is made of the same material as conventional composition shingles and is 36 inches wide, provides a quick, inexpensive roofing solution compared with shingling, although it helps to have an assistant. On the down side, roll roofing provides only one layer of covering (when used without underlayment) as opposed to the three layers that shingles provide.

The life of roll roofing is typically 5 to 12 years. Given its plain appearance and short life, single-layer roll roofing is best used on sheds or in places where the roof is not visible. It may be used on slopes that are flatter than those normally covered by shingles, especially if a concealed nail application is used. Double-coverage selvage roll roofing is used for roofs that are nearly flat.

Roll roofing is more fragile than other roofing options. In temperatures below 45 degrees the material may crack. You can work in colder conditions if you warm the rolls first. The roofing cement and lap cement must be kept at a temperature above 45 degrees, so store it indoors if you are working in cold weather.

Make sure the roofing has not curled at the edges or puckered in the middle. If it has, cut it into pieces 12 to 18 feet long and stack the pieces on a flat surface. Depending on the air temperature they will take an hour to one day to flatten.

Underlayment is not required, but since it is easy to install and so inexpensive, it is worth the extra effort. Install drip edge at the rakes and eaves before roofing. (See page 24.) Even small pebbles and sticks eventually poke through roll roofing, so sweep the surface with extra care.

Roll Roofing Option

An alternative to installing roll roofing horizontally to the rakes is to install it vertically. This eases the job when working on highly pitched roofs. Overlap pieces by 2 inches. Cement the seam, and nail every 3 inches. Horizontal seams (where a new piece of roll roofing continues the vertical run) also must overlap 2 inches. Cement the seam, and nail every 3 inches.

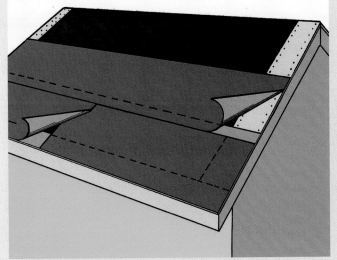

Installing Roll Roofing. Applied with nails and roofing cement, roll roofing is a quick and inexpensive option.

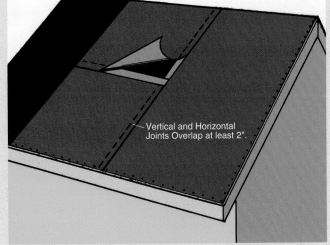

Vertical and Horizontal Joints Overlap at least 2".

Roll Roofing Option. An alternative for a highly pitched roof is to apply roll roofing parallel with the rake.

How To Install Roll Roofing

Exposed-Nail Method

The exposed-nail method is the quickest and easiest way to install roll roofing.

1 Installing the First Course. First, protect each valley with an 18-inch-wide sheet, taking extra care to lay it completely flat. If the material is raised above the sheathing, it will tear later if someone walks on it.

The eaves may be uneven, so do not use it as a guide for aligning the first sheet. Instead, snap a chalk line 35½ inches up from the eaves, and run your first sheet so that it overhangs the eaves by ½ inch. Add 2 inches of roofing cement at eaves, and nail all seams and edges every 3 inches. Use galvanized roofing nails to penetrate the sheathing by at least ¾ inch. Once you have "aimed" the sheet and put some nails down, you can't fix it if you find that it is headed off course. Avoid puckers and folds. Cut the course long enough so that some roofing overhangs the rake. When the roof is complete, use a utility knife to trim the course flush with the drip edge. If you are reroofing and there is no drip edge, strike a line so the new roofing can be trimmed flush with the previous layer.

2 Cementing and Nailing. Snap a chalk line 2 inches down from the top of the first sheet, and spread lap cement above this line. Roll out the next sheet, using the chalk line as a guide, and nail it. The cement seals all nails.

3 Cutting. At the rake edge of the roof, use the roll of roofing itself as a guide to a straight rough cut.

4 Covering Ridges and Hips. Cover ridges and hips after you have roofed both sides. Cut a piece of roll roofing 12 inches wide; snap chalk lines 6 inches down from the ridge on either side; apply lap cement above those lines; and nail down the ridge sheet.

1 Position roll roofing along the eaves overlapping the edge by ½ in. Align to a chalk line snapped 35½ in. from the bottom edge.

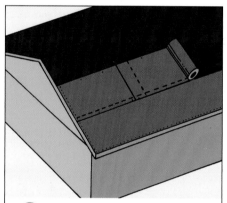

2 Strike a line 2 in. down from the top of the last course. Cement the seam, pressing down to ensure adhesion. Nail at 3-in. intervals.

3 Roll to the edge; then fold the roll back on itself. Use the roll as a cutting guide. Cut more roofing than needed, and trim as a final step.

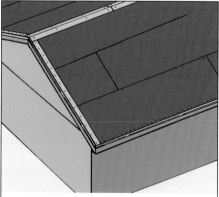

4 Cut a 12-in. piece of roll roofing. Snap chalk lines down from the ridge, and apply lap cement above those lines. Nail down the ridge roofing.

Doubling Up

For extra protection, use double layers of standard roll roofing. (For selvage roofing, see page 64.) Cut a 19-inch starter strip. Cement that strip to the deck, and nail it every 12 inches. Cover the starter strip with the first course; then lay the second course, leaving a 17-inch exposure. Apply roofing cement between layers, and nail only the area that will be overlapped. Lap roofing vertically 6 inches as needed, cementing and nailing every 2 inches where the overlap occurs.

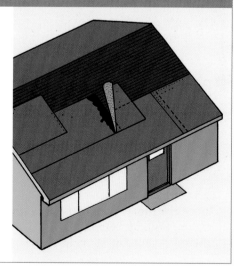

Concealed-Nail Method

The concealed-nail method is ideal for low-slope roofs (1 in 12 or less), where slow-moving water might work its way under nailheads.

1 **Adding Strips to Roof Edges.** When installing a new roof, begin by attaching 9-inch-wide starter strips of roll roofing along rakes and eaves. Use nails spaced 4 inches apart and ¾ inch from the edge. These strips provide a surface to which the cement adheres.

2 **Installing the First Course.** Snap a chalk line 35½ inches from the eaves as a guide for rolling out the first course of roofing. This allows the 36-inch-wide roll to overhang the eaves by ½ inch. Attach the first course to the chalk line, nailing the top edges only. Nail every 4 inches, ¾ inch from the top of the course. Trowel a rough 2-inch-wide layer of roofing cement under the first course at the eaves and the rake. Press down the seams to make sure they stick.

3 **Installing Remaining Courses.** Mark course overlaps as you go, by snapping a chalk line 6 inches down from the top of each course. Align the bottom of the next course, and nail along the top edge only. Then go back and apply roofing cement at the rakes and at the overlap with the course below.

4 **Covering Valleys.** Begin by covering each valley with an 18-inch-wide sheet of roll roofing. Be careful to lay it completely flat. As courses of roll roofing are added onto roofs adjacent to the valley, let each run 12 inches past the valley. Cement (do not nail) seams within 6 inches of the center of the valley. Then add roofing to the opposite face of the roof, again letting it overlap the valley. Trim down the center of the valley, and cement into place.

5 **Covering Ridges and Hips.** Ridges and hips are covered after both sides are roofed. Cut a piece of roll roofing 12 inches wide, and snap chalk lines 6 inches down. From the ridge on either side, apply lap cement above those lines, and seal down the ridge.

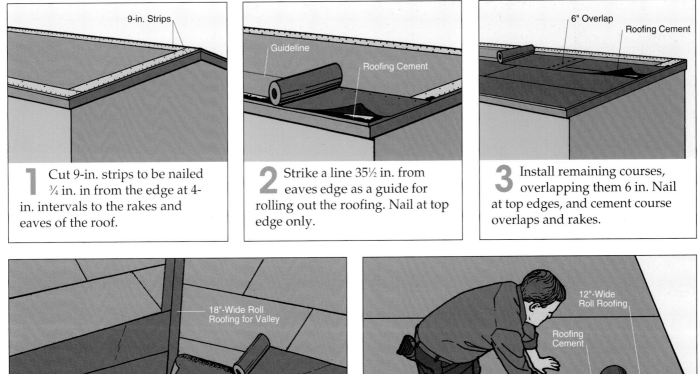

1 Cut 9-in. strips to be nailed ¾ in. in from the edge at 4-in. intervals to the rakes and eaves of the roof.

2 Strike a line 35½ in. from eaves edge as a guide for rolling out the roofing. Nail at top edge only.

3 Install remaining courses, overlapping them 6 in. Nail at top edges, and cement course overlaps and rakes.

4 After roofing the valley, add the courses of roofing so that courses overlap each other. Trim down the center of the valley.

5 Cover the ridge with a 12-in. strip sealed in place with roofing cement.

Double-Coverage Roll Roofing

Buy double coverage roll roofing (sometimes called selvage roofing) for those roofs that are nearly flat (up to 1 in 12). This material is applied with a 19-inch overlap called the selvage and 17-inch mineral-coated exposure. Selvage can be applied over shingle or roll roofing, although it is best to remove old roofing, repair the sheathing, and install drip edges. Each roll covers 51 square feet. Because of the thorough overlap, it provides a double layer of roofing. Be sure to purchase the type that is applied with cold cement rather than hot asphalt.

1 Applying the Starter Strip. Double coverage roofing is applied directly to sheathing. Cut away the 17-inch mineral-coated section to be used as the starter strip. Use a broom-handled brush to apply a 17-inch-wide layer of roofing cement along the eaves. Then press the starter strip into the cement, and roll it with a roofer's roller. (These can be rented.) Nail two rows of nails at 12-inch intervals across the the surface.

2 Adding the Course. Position the first course over the starter strip. Nail it in place, with two horizontal rows of nails. Position the rows 4½ inches and 13 inches from the top of the course. Space nails in rows about 12 inches apart. Roll back the sheet, and coat the selvage surface thickly with roofing cement.

3 Sealing Vertical Overlaps. Vertical seams are overlapped by 6 inches and are cemented rather than nailed. Nail the first sheet along the edge, spacing nails 4 inches apart and 1 inch in from the edge. Apply cement to the overlapping sheet, covering the first sheet 5½ inches in from its nailed edge. Nail the overlapping sheet in place (again nailing only on the selvage area). Press down the vertical seam for adhesion. Do not nail the exposed area.

4 Sealing Hips and Ridges. Finish hip and ridges by repeating the same procedure in miniature. Cut sections 12 inches wide from a roll of double coverage roofing. (Include both the selvage and exposed areas.) Snap a line, and apply a starter strip using only the selvage section of one piece. Nail the selvage section, spacing the nails at 4-inch intervals. Hammer one additional nail 1 inch in from the edge. Trowel on cement, and add the next section as you would a shingle. (See page 46.)

5 Trimming Rakes. As with roll roofing it is easiest to let the roofing overhang the rake and trim it when the roof is covered. Strike a line so that ¼ inch of roofing overhangs the drip edge. Use a hook blade utility knife to trim the rake.

1 Apply roofing cement along the eaves. Use the mineral-coated section as a starter strip.

2 Nail selvage of first full course. Apply cement under mineral-coated exposure.

3 Overlap vertical seams by 6 in. Apply cement, and seal. Nail the selvage area only.

4 Seal hips and ridges with a selvage section starter, and cement on next section.

5 Snap a chalk line, and use a utility knife to trim excess material at the rakes.

Built-Up Roofing

During the last 30 years many flat-roofed sections of homes, and in some cases whole homes, have been covered with a built-up roof (BUR). Do-it-yourselfers can easily patch built-up roofing. (See page 101.) Installing an entire built-up roof requires specialized equipment. If you have a built-up roof and foresee major repairs or replacement, you will want to know the components of built-up roofs and how to judge a professional crew.

Leaving It to the Professionals

Most built-up roofs are covered with three to five layers of heavy roofing felt coated with hot asphalt. A mineral surface of gravel or crushed rock often tops the job.

Depending on the number of layers applied and the way in which they are applied, a contractor guarantees the work for 10 to 20 years. If you hire a professional, make sure that a guarantee is in the contract.

Tools used by contractors range from simple mops and buckets to high-cost spraying equipment. The best job requires hot roofing, in which the asphalt coating is heated in large kettles before being applied. Built-up roofing is thick but not indestructible. When a roof begins to split or develops deep alligatoring (checked cracks that resemble alligator skin), it is time to have it inspected.

If serious alligatoring appears within a year or so of installation, the hot asphalt probably was laid too thickly and the job needs to be redone. Sometimes within several years of installation the roofing comes apart from the roof below or pulls away from other surfaces such as adjoining walls. (This is called delaminating.) These problems are caused when the surface of the roof is not completely cleared of debris or water before installation. If alligatoring or delaminating occurs, the roof must be redone.

Flashing Built-Up Roofs. The greatest potential for trouble is found in the places where the roof deck meets a vertical wall. A cant strip is placed in such a corner to soften the angle between roof and wall and to keep water from standing in the joint. Tile or metal flashing ideally overlaps the roofed surface.

Leaving it to the Professionals. Because of the need for applicators such as these, built-up roofing jobs are left to the professionals.

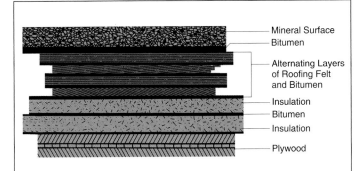

Mineral Surface
Bitumen
Alternating Layers of Roofing Felt and Bitumen
Insulation
Bitumen
Insulation
Plywood

Built-up Roofing. As its name implies, built-up roofing consists of several layers, beginning with plywood sheathing.

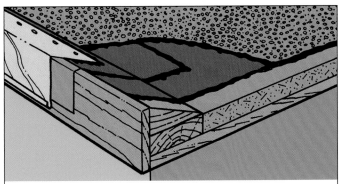

Flashing Built-up Roofs. Beveled strips of wood and a layer of flashing protects vulnerable joints.

chapter 6
other roofing

Panel Roofing

Corrugated panel roofs made of fiberglass provide a watertight, yet translucent covering for decks, carports, and greenhouses. In addition, corrugated aluminum and galvanized metal panels are easy to install and are long-lasting solutions for utility buildings. Panels of both types typically are sold along with manufacturer-specific nails, filler strips, and caulk. Install according to manufacturer's instructions.

Panel roofing is a quick and easy roofing solution, but keep in mind that fiberglass easily chips and metal tends to dent and bend—both are problems that cannot be fixed. The panels expand and contract with temperature changes and if not installed correctly this causes the roof to come detached. In addition to the roofing material, the job requires filler strips (pieces of wood shaped to fit the contours of the panels) and special nails (aluminum for aluminum roofs, steel for steel roofs) fitted with plastic washers.

1 Framing the Panel. Install 1x4 framing set on two-by rafters in accordance with local municipal codes. In areas of heavy snow, slope must be at least 8 in 12. No underlayment or drip edge is required. Panels also can be added over old roofing by applying 1x4 nailers every 2 to 4 feet. Use nails that penetrate the sheathing by at least ¾ inch.

2 Installing the Panels. In places where a complete seal against the weather is necessary, place filler strips under the roofing at the eaves. The strips are shaped to conform to the profile of the panels. Install the filler strips as you work your way across the the roof, beginning with the first full-width panel. Panels typically are 26 inches wide. Nail four nails across the panel where it rests on a framing piece. When working with steel and fiberglass, predrill a hole for each nail. Nail carefully so the roofing is snug to the framing but not indented. Overlap panels 1 inch lengthwise. Lay a bead of adhesive caulk across the length of each seam where panels overlap. For translucent fiberglass panels use clear silicone caulk. Panels are available in lengths up to 20 feet. If you need more than one panel from eaves to ridge, overlap by 12 inches on slopes greater than 4 in 12; 18 inches on lower slopes.

3 Installing Ridge Cap. Install ridge cap at ridges and hips. Some styles require filler strips, while others are shaped to fit the roofing. Nail at ridges according to the manufacturer's recommended pattern. Do not nail edges that will be overlapped. Overlap panels with the ridge cap by at least an inch. Overlap sections of ridge panel by 6 inches.

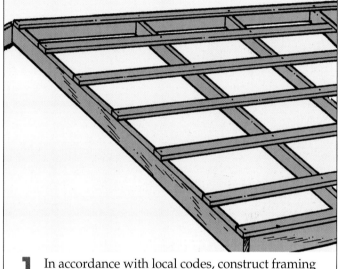

1 In accordance with local codes, construct framing out of 1x4s.

2 Allow panels to overhang rake by ¼ to ⅜ in., and eaves by 2 in. Overlap panels side-by-side 1 in.

3 Install ridge cap at ridges and hips. Some styles require filler strips while others are shaped to fit the roofing. Overlap panels with the ridge cap by 1 in.

6 Other Roofing

Slate Roofing

Slate is an expensive roofing option with a very long life (from 50 to 100 years). Nothing else provides the rugged-yet-classy look of slate. Slate can be placed over a layer of composition shingles only if the slope of the roof is 4 in 12 or more and only if a structural engineer has confirmed the roof framing can bear slate's 7-pound-per-square-foot weight. Slating is a skill that demands considerable investment both in time and money—an investment better put toward the cost of hiring a professional.

Slate is stone that has been mined from the ground and cut to size. It is available in a wide variety of grades and thicknesses, so ask a salesman how long your selection is expected to last. Slate comes in many colors, from gray to shades of green, purple, and red. Some colors fade after years of exposure. Slate also can be smooth or rough surfaced.

Slate is heavy. Just how heavy depends on the grade. Be sure your roof can handle the load. Many local codes require specific reinforcements if you want to put slate over an existing roof. Copper flashing is recommended because it is long-lasting and looks good with slate.

The professionals use three simple but specialized tools: a nail ripper, which is used to cut off a nail level to the surface; a hammer equipped with a sharp edge for cutting slate and a point for poking nailholes in the slate; and a T-bar which aids in trimming the pieces of slate.

Synthetic Slate. If you love the look of slate but you do not have the money to put into it, you can use a compromise material. New varieties of slate lookalikes made of a variety of materials are light and attractive. These new products not only look a lot like slate, but they also share much of its durability and are worth investigating. As with slate, they are typically contractor installed.

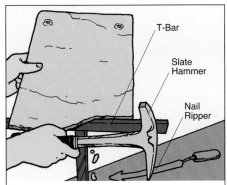

Slate Roofing. Applying a slate roof requires three specialized tools: A nail ripper, a hammer equipped with a sharp edge and a point, and a T-bar for trimming.

Installing Slate

The following list outlines the basic procedures used for installing a slate roof.

1. Shimming the Starter Course. Slate tilts slightly upward at the eaves, extending ½ inch beyond the rake and 1 inch beyond the eaves. Use a piece of lath to shim the starter course, which is made up of slates set lengthwise.

2. Installing Felt Underlayment. Slate often is laid on one layer of 30-pound roofing felt. Some contractors prefer to use individual felt strips under each course to provide additional cushioning.

3. Installing the Slates. Two nails, installed in pre-punched holes, hold each slate. The slates are set so their beveled edges show. There is a ¹⁄₁₆-inch gap between slates.

4. Offsetting the Gaps. The gaps between slates are offset by at least 2 inches.

5. Capping the Ridge. The ridge is capped with slates that are the same width. The overlap at the peak is alternated from one side of the roof to the other. Slates are fastened to the ridge with two nails.

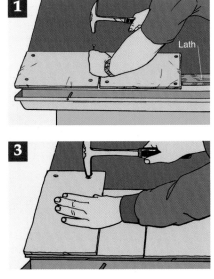

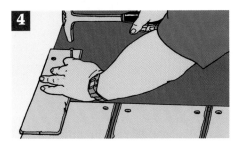

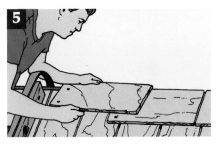

Working with Slate

■ Use solid copper- or zinc-coated nails. These are nailed through factory-punched holes in each slate.

■ Give slate roofs extra pitch (called canting) at the eaves. Before slating, a ¼-inch-thick strip of wood is nailed along the eaves. This causes the bottom course of slate to turn upwards slightly. It also gives the roof a classic appearance and provides additional drip protection for the fascia.

■ To prevent cracking the slate courses, use proper scaffolding. (Or make sure your contractor uses proper scaffolding.)

■ Slate nails do not penetrate metal flashing. Unlike the nails used with shingle roofs, these nails have no way of sealing themselves.

■ Use plenty of roofing cement under hip and ridge slates. All exposed nailheads also must be covered with cement.

■ Slates must lap over the underlying course by at least 3 inches.

■ Slates with hairline cracks should be discarded; cracks only worsen over time.

Maintaining and Repairing Slate

There is little maintenance involved when it comes to a slate roof. The only thing you have to worry about is debris that traps moisture along eaves and degrades the slate. Broken slates can be replaced, but you will need a slate ripper to remove the damaged portion.

1 Clipping Nails. Slip the nail under the slate to be replaced. Hook the ripper onto the shaft of a nail that holds the slate in place. Hammer the ripper to cut the nail. Repeat with the second nail to release the slate.

2 Cutting a Replacement. Cut slate to size with a carborundum circular saw blade. Or use a nail set to punch a series of holes along the cut line; snap the slate on the edge of a hard surface, such as a bench. Wear goggles.

3 Marking Nailholes. Slip a new slate into the space, and mark for nailholes in the crack between shingles in the overlapping course. If two cracks overlap the replacement shingle, make a mark at both. Drill holes using a ⅛-inch masonry bit.

4 Nailing the Gap. Put back the slate and use a nail set to gently drive an 8d galvanized finishing nail.

5 Covering the Nailhead. Gently pry up the overlapping slates. Cut a piece of copper roughly 5 x 6 inches, and bend it until it is slightly cupped. Slip the cupped copper sheet over the nailhead to seal it. Friction holds the sheet in place.

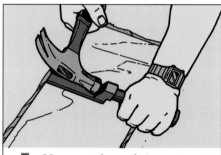

1 Hammer the nail ripper to cut the nails holding a damaged shingle.

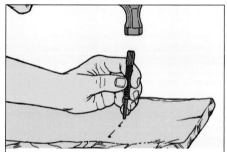

2 To cut slate, punch a series of holes on the back of the slate and then sever along the line.

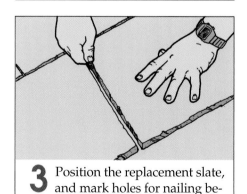

3 Position the replacement slate, and mark holes for nailing between the overlapping shingles.

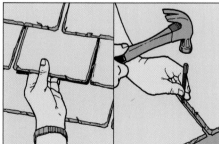

4 Replace the slate, and use a nail set to drive galvanized nails flush with the slate surface.

5 Gently pry up overlapping shingles, and slip in a cupped piece of copper over the nailhole.

Tile Roofing

Like slate, classic clay tiles last from 50 to 100 years and possess a timeless quality few other materials have to offer. Tiles also are expensive and very heavy, weighing as much as 1,000 pounds to the square. Concrete tiles are a smart substitute. They look good, last almost as long as clay tiles, and are light enough to be installed on some standard roofs intended for composition shingles.

If you are considering a tile or concrete tile roof, consult your roofing supply source and local building department to make sure your roof can handle the tiles you choose. Do not tile over a roof that has a slope flatter than 3 in 12.

Although more difficult to apply than shingles, tiles can be installed by a skilled do-it-yourselfer. In addition to the tools used for installing composition shingles, you also will need a circular saw with a masonry-cutting blade.

Caution: Wear protective goggles when cutting tiles.

If you can fit it into your budget, use copper nails rather than galvanized nails. An advantage to using copper nails is that they are soft enough to cut through should you have to replace a tile. Copper nails also allow enough give so that if you nail them too far into the tiles, the tiles will not crack as the decking moves with temperature variations. Hammer all nails, no matter what kind, to within a nickel's thickness of the tile surface.

Preparing the Deck

Although there are various ways to install tile, a few basics prevail. Your tiles will come with instructions pertaining to whether or not they require underlayment. Some tiles are nailed directly to sheathing, while others require battens to be laid first. Battens are 1x2 strips of redwood or pressure-treated pine that are spaced at intervals that match the tile exposure. (14 inches is typical.) Further preparations also

may be called for, such as one 2x2 along all ridges and hips, 1x2 starter strips along eaves and rakes, or 1x3 nailed to rake rafters to allow the tiles to extend further sideways. Check manufacturer's instructions.

Use flashing that will last as long as your tiles. Copper is best. Apply metal drip edge along the eaves before the underlayment (if any) is installed. Along the rakes, the drip edge is installed after the underlayment. Take special care in the valleys; first put down 90-pound mineral-surfaced roll roofing, then W-metal that is at least 24 inches wide. (See page 25.) Cover hips and ridges with a double layer of felt.

Tile Alternatives. Tiles are designed to interlock so the amount of exposure is always readily apparent. Nail them down to the sheathing or "hang" them on the battens. If your roof has a slope of 7 in 12 or steeper or if you live in an area subject to high winds, fasten every third or fourth course with metal clips.

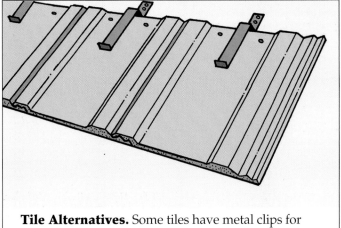

Tile Alternatives. Some tiles have metal clips for additional hanging support.

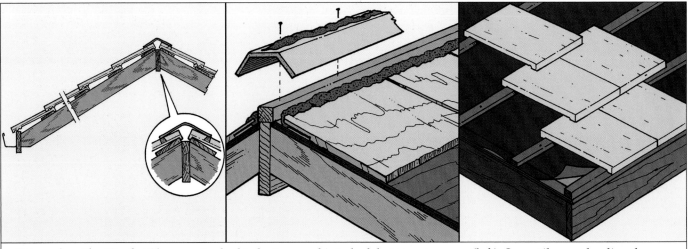

Preparing the Deck. Tiles are attached to battens and interlock between courses (left). Some tiles can be directly attached to roof sheathing. The ridge is sealed with mortar and a cap (center). Concrete tiles lock onto 1x2 battens attached to the decking (right).

1. Setting the Tile Width. The positioning of the tiles is crucial. (You cannot end at a rake with half a tile.) Snap a chalk line as a guide along the eaves. Tiles hang over the eaves by 2 inches. Nail the gable rake tiles in place, overlapping the drip edge. By dividing the total length of the eaves by the width of a tile, determine the distance each tile will be set apart and mark the drip edge accordingly. Tiles provide about 1 inch of sideways leeway where they overlap the previous tile. Set the eaves closure tiles flush with the eaves edge and nail in place.

2. Setting the Tile. Apply roofing mastic where one tile overlaps the other. Set the first tile in place, and nail with a 6d nail.

3. Nailing the First Course. Install six tiles using the marks along the rake and the horizontal chalk line as positioning guides. Double-check your width calculation to make sure the course ends with a full-width tile.

4. Adding the Second Course. Work up the roof in stair-step fashion. Overlap the tiles by at least 3 inches.

5. Finishing the Course. Lay the left-hand rake tiles. Toenail a 1x3 nailer that runs from eaves to ridge. Position it so that it lines up with holes in the tile that are provided for nailing. Nail the last tile of each course to this nailer.

6. Laying the Ridge. Lay a bed of tinted mortar, and set ridge starter tiles. Apply the hip and ridge tiles over the ridge, overlapping each by at least 3 inches.

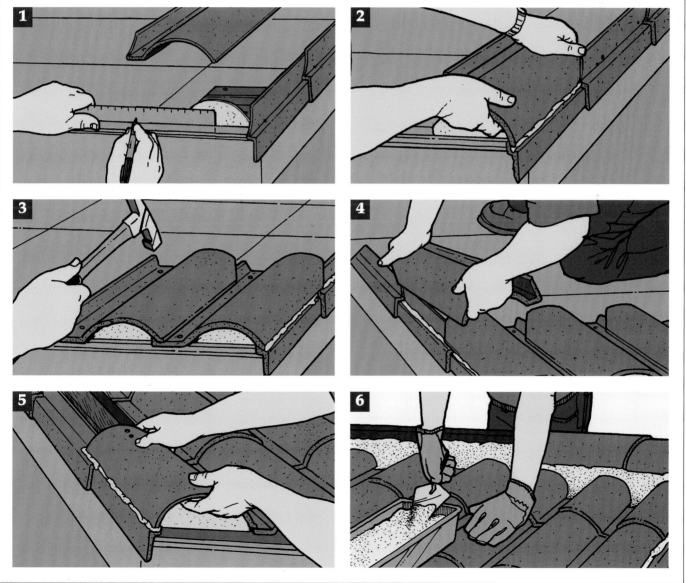

6 Other Roofing

Metal Roofing

The metal roof is experiencing new popularity. This may be due to the success of metal roofs on commercial buildings, or perhaps the historical appropriateness of metal roofing on older homes. Metal boasts a longevity surpassed only by slate and tile—at a considerably lower cost.

Standing-seam panel roofing is the most common type of metal roofing for residential use. These panels, which run vertically, usually are made of aluminum or galvanized steel, but in some cases they are made of zinc and aluminum-coated steel. Because the panels are painted, they offer more color options than other types of roofing. Metal roofing is ideal for restoring older homes that originally had metal roofs.

This light material (one pound per square foot) is suitable for covering old roofs and may even be used over three layers of composition shingles (if local codes permit). For roofs that have irregularities, narrow, textured and dull-finish panels are best.

The metal roofing shown here can cover a roof with a slope of at least 3 in 12. Other metal roof systems handle roofs with slopes as slight as ¼-inch in 12 (usually a job for built-up roofing). However, the experience and special equipment of a contractor is needed for its installation.

The installation process involves laying 12- to 16½-inch panels and correctly joining them at the seams, wall flashing, valleys, and ridges. The panels are precut to the exact length ordered up to 40 feet long. (For this reason horizontal seams are very unlikely on most homes.) Metal roofing can be applied to plywood decking with an underlayment of 30-pound felt. Laying and joining the panels is not difficult, but handling eaves edges, rakes, wall flashing valleys, and ridges requires experience.

Working with a Professional

Before committing to a contractor, check his/her references and make sure he/she is certified to install the material you have chosen. Visit nearby sites and use the following tips to help evaluate the contractor:

Use of Sealant. Tape sealant is used within joints, but almost never on the surface where it can be seen (and where it can wear off with time). Too much reliance on sealant might be a sign that the contractor is not installing the material correctly. Expect some visible sealant in places where ridge panels join and around the vent stack sleeves.

Signs of Quality Work. Check that panels are straight, and that details at the rakes and eaves are neat. Denting, particularly in the valley, is a sign of poor craftsmanship. Check that stack penetrations are neat and that minimal sealant is used on them.

Check for Other Metals. Lead stack sleeves, steel antenna wires, and copper gutters all contain a metal that corrodes the roofing. An experienced contractor knows to replace these problem items.

Few Exposed Fasteners. The standing seam system has exposed fasteners only on the rake and eaves trim, and then only sparingly. If exposed fasteners are used, they must be coated, long-life fasteners.

Get the Manual. Manufacturers want their systems to be applied correctly and most will not hesitate to send you a manual. Use it as a guide to asking the right questions.

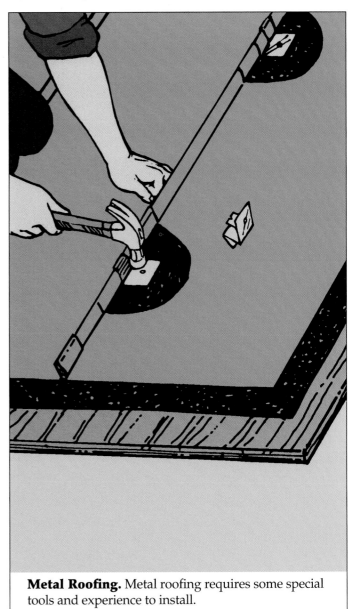

Metal Roofing. Metal roofing requires some special tools and experience to install.

As mentioned, installing metal roofing requires some special tools and experience. Here's an overview of what is involved.

1. Installing Felt and Eaves Trim. Thirty-pound felt provides a moisture barrier over plywood decking. Metal roofing is applied vertically, completing a 12- to 16½-inch panel from eaves to ridge before applying the next. Check the squareness of the roof, and adjust for irregularity. Eaves trim is screwed in place, and sealant is applied to the edge before panels are clipped in place.

2. Applying the First Rake Edge. After the first vertical panel has been set, the first rake edge (applied on either side of the roof, depending on the installer's preference) is applied over the panel. Underlayment overlaps the rake edge.

3. Joining the Panels. Clips and sealant join the panels. Clips are applied every 12 inches where high winds prevail, every 18 inches elsewhere. No adhesive is necessary to seal the sheets to the decking. Do not step on the seams. In fact, walk on the sheets as little as possible. Scratched finishes may void the warranty.

4. Installing Valley Flashing. Valley flashing is set on a piece of 30-pound felt underlayment that lines the valley. Channels running parallel with the valley are sealed and screwed to it and hold the edge of the panels.

5. Sealing Ridge Flashing. At the ridges, flashing is sealed to "Z" strips that are fastened between the standing seams.

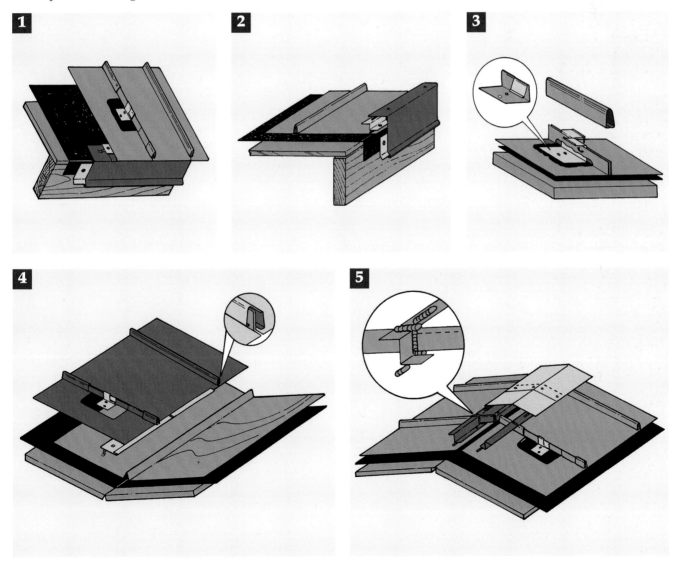

chapter 7
ventilating roofs

Ventilating the Roof

Whether the attic space is insulated from above or below, adequate ventilation coming from the underside of the roof deck must be provided. Ventilation allows heat to escape, preventing ice buildups on the eaves in winter and an overheated roof in summer. Ice buildups damage the structure and cause water leaks inside the house. (See "Preventing Ice Dams," page 81.)

To ventilate a roof, make a path for air to get into and out of the space between the roof deck and the insulation. To ensure air movement, locate the intake port at a low point on the roof and the exhaust port at a high point.

Incoming Air. The most effective way to provide ventilation is through vents that are placed in the soffits (which are found at the lowest points on the roof). Continuous soffit strip vents provide the most reliable port for intake air, while rectangular vents are next on the list. Round ventilator plugs are easy to install, but usually are too small to provide adequate airflow. Insulation baffles compress the insulation near the eaves and ensure a clear pathway for air to travel between the rafters.

Outgoing Air. Stale air escapes through the top of the roof through gable vents on the end walls, turbine vents on the roof, or ridge vents, also found on the roof. Continuous ridge vents are the preferred type for pitched roofs, while gravity vents are best installed where ridge vents are not feasible, such as in a hip roof. For houses that have open attics and insulated attic floors, vents located in the gable ends may suffice if the openings are large enough. Gable vents also can be used for ventilation in a finished attic above an insulated flat ceiling.

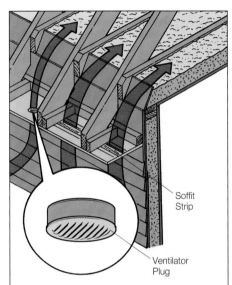

Incoming Air. The best way to let air into the roof is through soffit vents. Ventilator plugs, continuous soffit strip vents, and rectangular vents are most often used.

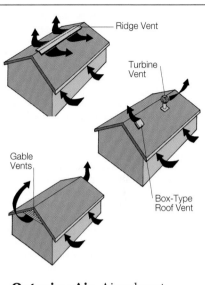

Outgoing Air. Air exhaust options include ridge vents, turbines, box-type vents, and gable vents.

Calculating Adequate Roof Ventilation

The amount of area needed to provide for roof ventilation depends on whether or not the ceiling has a vapor barrier. If there is a vapor barrier allow one square foot of free ventilating area for every 300 square feet of house area. If there is no vapor barrier, double the ventilating area. The total free ventilating area must be divided equally between the intake and exhaust ports. Because the thickness of vanes or wires in a venting device reduces the airspace, use oversized vents to compensate. For example, if the vent has a screen with 1/8-inch-square holes, divide the area of the screen by 1.25 to get the free ventilating area. If the vents used consist of louvers backed by screens, divide by 2.25. The following example shows how to size soffit and ridge vents for a 25 x 40-foot house that has a vapor barrier in the ceiling:

1. Figure the area of the attic under the roof: 25 multiplied by 40 equals 1000 square feet.

2. The free ventilating area equals 1000 divided by 300, or 3.33 square feet. To convert feet to inches, multiply 3.33 by 144 to get 479.52 square inches. You need half of this amount (239.76 square inches) for the soffit vents and the other half for the ridge vents.

3. Each 8 x 12-inch louvered soffit vent used has an area of 96 square inches. Divide this number by 2.25 to get 43 square inches (rounded off) of free area. The number of vents needed is 239.76 square inches divided by 43, which is 5.58, rounded off to 6. Use three on each side of the roof.

4. The product literature that comes with the ridge vent provides information concerning the necessary free ventilating area per lineal foot. One rolled ridge vent product yields 17 inches, so the house in this example needs a strip equal to the free area required at the ridge: 239.76 square inches divided by 17 equals 14 feet.

Ventilating Unheated Attics

Unheated attics are the easiest type to ventilate. Air enters through vents in the eaves, rises naturally toward the roof deck, and exits through a continuous vent on the ridge, gable vents on the end walls, or roof vents placed high on the roof. If an airway is maintained under the roof (where the ceiling insulation abuts the eaves), the moving air keeps the roof ventilated, but does not affect the insulated ceiling below.

An unheated attic is ventilated easily by installing soffit vents for air to come in and a ridge vent, gable vent, or roof vent for air to escape.

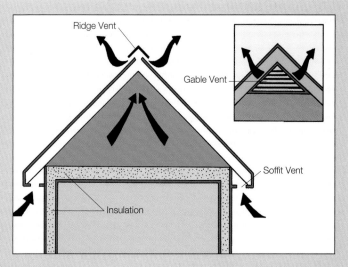

Ventilating Heated Attics

Providing ventilation in a heated attic is a bit trickier than working with an unheated one, but the same principles apply. The important thing is to maintain at least 2 inches of clearance between the underside of the roof deck and all insulation. This allows the air to travel from the eaves to the top of the roof. If the eaves provide a space of 10 inches or more, simply choose insulation that has a thickness that allows for this additional 2-inch airspace. Most likely though, a combination of blanket insulation between the rafters and rigid insulation attached to the underside of the rafters will be necessary to achieve the desired R-value, while retaining an adequate amount of airspace.

Leave a 2-in. airspace between the insulation and roof deck to allow air to go from intake to exhaust vents.

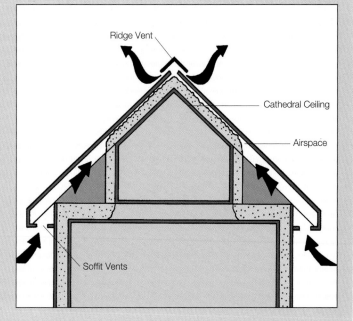

Ventilating Cathedral Ceilings

Like the roof deck above heated attics, cathedral ceilings must contain an airspace above insulated cavities. Unlike attics, however, not every cathedral ceiling has an easy escape port such as a roof ridge. If not, other ways must be designed to allow air to escape. Special roof vents are available for cathedral ceilings and almost any other special conditions, such as a low roof that abuts a vertical wall.

Special roof-to-wall vents provide ventilation in places where the roof abuts a wall.

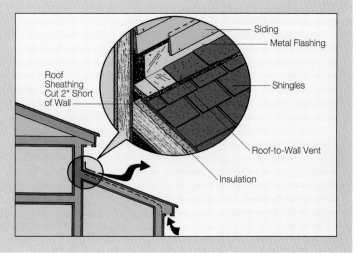

Rectangular and Plug Soffit Vents

Continuous soffit strip ventilators work well and are easy to install into a new soffit. However, installing them into an existing soffit often requires tearing the soffit apart. Two better options in this case include rectangular soffit vents and ventilator plugs, or plug soffit vents.

Installing Rectangular Soffit Vents

Those who decide to use rectangular soffit vents can use the guidelines found in "Calculating Adequate Roof Ventilation" on page 75 to determine the size and quantity needed at each soffit.

1 **Drilling a Starter Hole.** Mark the location of the vent on the soffit and, using a ¾-inch drill bit, drill a starter hole at one corner of the marked rectangle.

2 **Cutting the Opening.** Insert the blade of a saber saw into the starter hole, and cut the opening.

3 **Attaching the Vent.** Secure the vent to the soffit using the screws that are supplied with the vent. An electric drill equipped with a Phillips bit makes the job a lot easier.

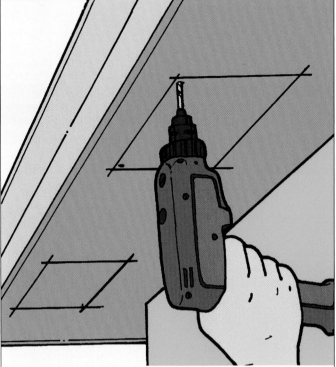

1 Use the vent as a template to mark the cutouts. Use a ¾-in. drill bit to drill a starter hole at one corner of the marked box.

2 Insert the blade of a saber saw into the starter hole, and cut the opening.

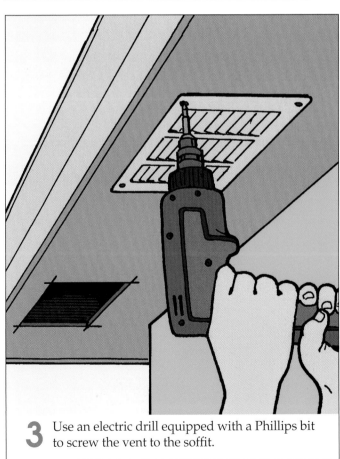

3 Use an electric drill equipped with a Phillips bit to screw the vent to the soffit.

Installing Plug Soffit Vents

Ventilator plugs usually do not yield the free area required by the guidelines on page 75, but it is better to use them than to have no ventilation at all. Use at least two plugs per rafter bay.

1 Cutting Holes. Each rafter bay requires two holes. Mark the center of each hole, and use an electric drill equipped with a hole saw bit to cut a 2½-inch-diameter hole. If you do not have an electric drill, mark off the outline of the hole, drill a starter hole on the edge, and use a keyhole or saber saw to cut the hole.

2 Inserting the Plug. Push an aluminum or plastic plug into the hole until the flange is flush with the soffit.

1 Mark the center of each hole, and use an electric drill equipped with a hole saw bit to cut a 2½-in. diameter hole.

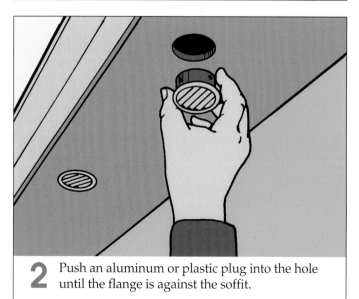

2 Push an aluminum or plastic plug into the hole until the flange is against the soffit.

Ridge Vents

Ridge vents come as rigid lengths of metal (top), composite materials (middle), or in rolls of an air-permeable material (bottom). The lower two are designed to accept roof shingles.

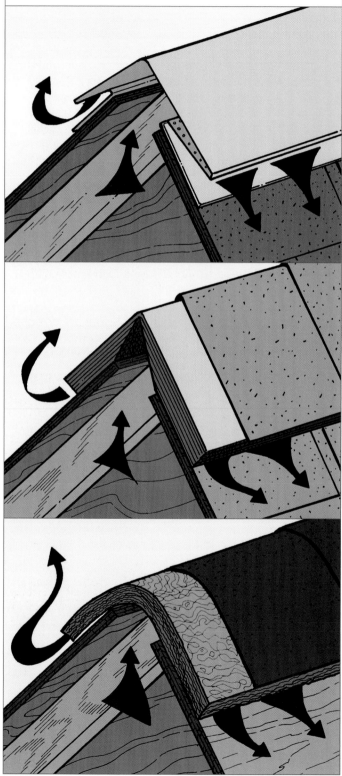

Installing a Ridge Vent

Ridge vents are made of various materials and may be packaged in rigid sections or rolls. A well-designed vent allows air to escape, but keeps out rain and snow. Because the ridge vent sits on top of the roof, it is highly visible. Keep this in mind when choosing a vent. Many homeowners opt for one that can have shingles installed on top.

1 Cutting an Opening. Use a circular saw with a carbide-tipped blade to cut a 2-inch slot along each side of the ridge. Start the cut 6 inches from one end of the ridge, and end it 6 inches from the other end. Set the blade depth to cut through the roofing and sheathing only, leaving the rafters uncut.

Caution: Wear goggles and make sure you have solid footing when cutting with a saw. Install roofing cleats if necessary to support yourself on the roof. Lay out the extension cord so that there is no chance of tripping on it.

2 Attaching the Vent. Uncoil the vent (if it's packaged in rolls) or secure a rigid vent to the ridge. Extend the vent to cover the uncut 6-inch portions of roof at each end. If you're using a metal vent that is not intended to be topped with shingles, nail the flanges to the roof using aluminum roofing nails.

3 Topping the Vent. For ridge vents that are designed to be covered with shingles, cut three ridge shingles from one three-tab composition shingle. Place the first

shingle over one end of the ridge vent, aligning it with the edge of the shingles along the roof rake. Nail the shingle through the part to be covered by the next shingle. Using roofing nails that are long enough to penetrate into the sheathing, install one nail at each side of the ridge. Put the next shingle in place over the nails, and continue.

1 Cut a 2-in.-wide slot along each side of the ridge, leaving 6 in. of each end uncut.

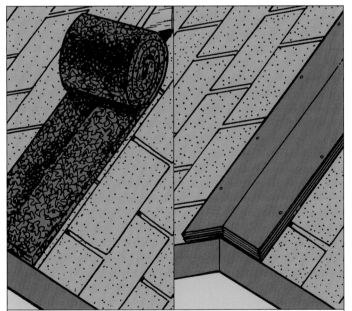

2 Uncoil a rolled vent (left) or secure a rigid vent (right) along the slot and over the uncut ends of the roof.

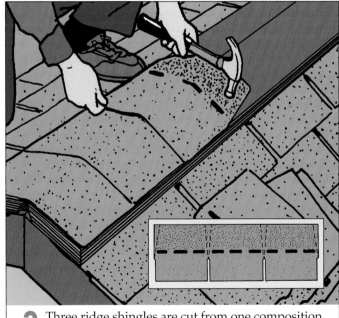

3 Three ridge shingles are cut from one composition shingle (inset). Place ridge shingles over the top of the vent. Without compressing the vent material, drive the nails through the shingles and vent and into the sheathing.

Installing a Box-Type Gravity Roof Vent

While ridge vents are the preferred way to create an escape outlet near the top of a roof, they are not easy to install on some houses. For example, ridge vents are not suited to houses that have hip roofs. Instead, one or more gravity vents usually are installed.

Turbine vents are a type of gravity vent that have vanes located in the turbine-shaped top of the vent, which usher air to the outside. When there is a breeze the vanes move, increasing the capacity of the device by an average of 130 percent. The downside to turbine vents, other than their prominent appearance, is a tendency to ice up in winter. Some homeowners prevent this by cloaking them in garbage bags in winter; a measure that prevents them from working when they are most needed.

Box-type gravity vents do not have moving parts. They have louvers on all sides but the top. The step-by-step instructions for installing them are the same for turbine vents.

1 Cutting an Opening. Drive a nail through the roof sheathing from the attic below to locate a clear opening between framing. Using the nail as a guide, mark an opening the same size as the throat opening of the vent. Then remove the nail and use a carbide-tipped saw blade to cut out the opening.

Caution: Wear goggles and make sure you have solid footing when cutting with a saw. Install roofing cleats if necessary to support yourself on the roof. Lay out the extension cord so that there is no chance of tripping on it.

2 Adjusting the Roofing. Use a utility knife that has a hooked blade to cut and remove shingles so that the top of the roof vent slides under the two topmost shingle courses. Use a pry bar to pull out nails that may interfere when sliding the vent under the courses. Before placing the vent, apply roofing cement around the cut opening and under the point at which it will contact the flange.

3 Installing the Vent. Slide the vent under the top two shingle courses and over the bottom two courses. Then lift up the shingles and, using nails made of the same metal as the flange, nail the vent through the flange.

4 Sealing the Roof. Apply roofing cement using either a stick from a gallon-sized container or, better, a cartridge in a caulking gun. Press each shingle firmly into place. Finally, lay a bead of caulk around the joint between the shingles and the flange of the vent.

1 Drive a nail through the roof sheathing to determine where to make the cut. Mark an opening the same size as the throat opening of the vent. Use a carbide-tipped saw blade to cut the opening.

2 Remove shingles so that the top of the vent can slide under the two topmost courses. Use a pry bar to remove nails. Apply roofing cement around the cut opening.

3 Slide the vent under the top two shingle courses and over the bottom two. Lift up the shingles, and use galvanized or aluminum nails to nail through the flange around the vent.

4 Apply roofing cement under each shingle and press it firmly into place. Apply a bead of caulk around the joint between the shingles and the vent flange.

Preventing Ice Dams

There are several possible solutions to ice-dam problems. Working from the outside, you can install a strip of sheet metal over the shingles covering the overhang. This method is fairly common in the rural Northeast—it is most effective on steeply sloped roofs, where gravity and the slick metal surface encourage ice and snow to slide off the roof.

Another approach is to install heat cables in a zigzag pattern along the shingles on the overhang. The resistance wiring, which looks like a long extension cord, is attached with small clips tucked under the shingles and even can be extended into gutters to help them remain unfrozen. These cables are designed to produce enough heat to prevent freeze-ups.

Because warmth rising through the ceiling or attic is often the cause of ice dams, you can also alleviate the problem by working from the inside to reduce the heat flow with extra insulation. In a typically constructed wood frame attic floor, for instance, the spaces between floor joists should be filled with insulation. An additional layer, even the 3½-inch batting used in walls, can be set on top of and perpendicular to the joists for more protection. At the same time you can increase the vent size in the attic or crack a window at each end. This will make the bottom of the roof colder and closer to the temperature outdoors, which will prevent melting, while the extra insulation will retard heat flow from living spaces below.

On new construction jobs or reroofing projects, consider installing a rubberized ice shield membrane on the roof deck. It should cover the overhang and the sheathing under at least a few courses of shingles over living space. This provides a backup barrier just in case an ice dam does form and works under the shingles.

Usually, these membranes are made of waterproof, rubberized asphalt and polyethylene in self-adhering sheets that bond directly to the roof deck and to each other at overlaps. The material is installed beneath the shingles, and it seals itself around punctures from nails protruding through the shingles above.

Ice Dams

Ice dams form as snow on the roof melts and then refreezes along the eaves. Even in houses with insulation in the ceilings, enough heat can rise through the blankets or batts to gradually warm the bottom of the roof over the attic if there is inadequate air flow or attic ventilation. In the right conditions, the heat causes the snow blanket to melt from the bottom up, and water trickles down toward the gutter. It may be cold outside, but the trickle is protected from freezing by the snow above. When the melted water reaches the roof overhang, there is no longer a heat source from below because the overhang is outside the exterior wall. That's where the water begins to freeze. It forms a dam, and the water above can back up under shingles.

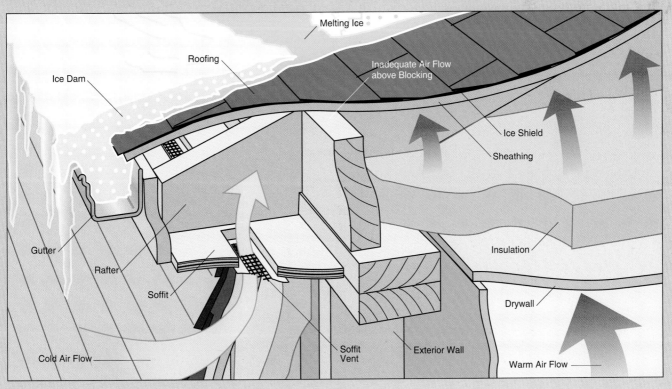

Melting Ice · Roofing · Ice Dam · Inadequate Air Flow above Blocking · Ice Shield · Sheathing · Insulation · Gutter · Rafter · Soffit · Drywall · Soffit Vent · Exterior Wall · Warm Air Flow · Cold Air Flow

roofing projects

Dormers

Building a dormer may seem like a small project, but it actually calls for a diverse collection of construction skills—many of the same skills necessary to build an entire house. Still, building a dormer or two is well worth the effort for those who desire additional natural light, ventilation, and a way to make the most of existing floor space.

Types of Dormers

Dormers change the roofline of the house and provide headroom where it's needed most (near the eaves). Because they're visible outside the house, you'll want the dormers to complement the style of the house.

Gable Dormers. A gable dormer has a roof with two pitched planes that meet at a ridge. The ceiling is usually vaulted. The roof pitch need not match that of the house, but it may help the dormer fit in better visually. A valley at the intersection of the dormer roof and the surrounding roof channels away water. A gable dormer is good for creating natural light and ventilation.

Shed Dormers. The hallmark of a shed dormer is its single flat roof, which is pitched at less of an angle than that of the existing roof. This kind of roof is easier to build than the roof on a gable dormer. It's also easier to join to the existing roof because shingles simply lap over the intersection. The ceiling inside a shed dormer either follows the upward slope of the rafters or is totally flat. The best feature of a shed dormer, however, is that it dramatically increases the usable floor space in an attic. As an option, you may want to add shed dormers on both sides of the roof, an arrangement that resembles saddlebags.

Eyebrow Dormers. Unlike other types of dormers, an eyebrow is used primarily to allow natural light into an attic or to serve as a decorative accent for certain house styles. Its small size and curved shape encourage the use of a fixed, rather than operable, window. The window itself is usually custom-made, but some manufacturers offer a limited selection of stock units.

A modified shed dormer creates a small alcove in this garage apartment.

Planning a Dormer

There are several things to consider when deciding on the size and style of your dormer. For one, the dormer must be built in proportion to the house: a king-size dormer on a small roof causes the house to appear top-heavy, while a dormer that's too small doesn't admit a worthwhile amount of light.

Before you cut a hole in the roof, draw a section view (cross section, or side view) of the existing attic framing.

1 **Measure the Slope.** The slope of a roof is traditionally expressed as the number of inches it "rises" for every foot it "runs." Rise is measured vertically; run is measured horizontally. Use a level and tape measure to determine slope. Mark the level at a point 12 inches from one end; then hold the level against the underside of a rafter until it reads level. Use the tape to measure the distance from the level to the rafter at the 12-inch mark. If the distance from the rafter to the level is 11 inches, for example, the slope is 11 inches of rise in 12 inches of run. This is written as 11/12. Carpenters often express it as "11 in 12." Some electronic levels can provide a direct readout of roof slope.

2 **Draw a Cross Section.** Measure the width of the gable end, the outdoor height of its walls, the depth of the rafters, and the depth of the attic floor joists. Use this information, along with the slope of the roof found in Step 1, to draw a cross section of the house to scale.

3 **Design the Dormer.** Place a sheet of tracing paper over the drawing made in Step 2, or make photocopies of the drawing. Sketch a rafter first; then experiment with various locations for the dormer's face wall. For a shingle roof to drain properly, the rafters must have a slope of at least 3 in 12. The rafter can extend all the way to the existing ridge, if necessary. Measure from the attic floor to the underside of the dormer rafters to determine the headroom that results. Add details such as the header and plate for the window; this is essentially a cross-sectional view of the window's rough opening. Make sure you include at least a double 2x6 header. The bottom of the rough opening must be at least 6 inches above the plane of the roof for flashing and window trim.

Once the construction details of the dormer are worked out, you might want to see how it will look on your house. One way to do this is to make a scale drawing of the front of the house, then draw in the dormer, along with its window. Another way is to take a photo of the house and use a permanent marker to draw the dormer on it. Take a photo that includes both the front and one gable end of the house (a three-quarter view), allowing you to sketch in both the front and the side of the dormer.

1 Before building, determine the roof slope using a level and tape measure (top) or an electronic level (inset).

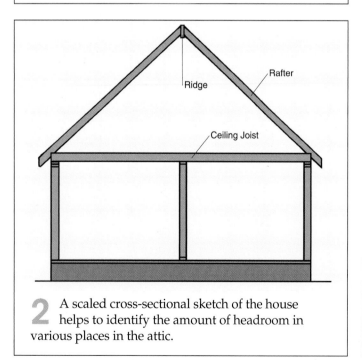

2 A scaled cross-sectional sketch of the house helps to identify the amount of headroom in various places in the attic.

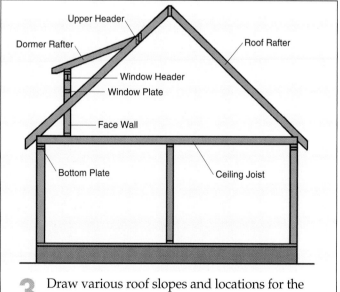

3 Draw various roof slopes and locations for the face wall. Ask an engineer whether the joists can support the dormer.

Building a Shed Dormer

You have to cut a large opening in the existing roof to build a dormer, so be sure to have all the necessary tools and materials (including windows) on hand before you start. Being prepared minimizes the amount of time that the house is vulnerable to changes in the weather. Purchase a heavy-duty waterproof tarp to cover the opening overnight or in the event of unexpected rain. Once the dormer is tight to the weather, you can finish the inside. Building a dormer requires that you spend a lot of time on the main roof, though much of the construction is actually done from inside the attic. Roof work is hazardous. To minimize the risk of injury and to help the work proceed smoothly, be sure to have a stable work platform.

1 **Establish the Opening.** If you haven't done so already, install plywood subflooring throughout the attic. This provides a safe platform from which to build the dormer and keeps demolition debris out of the floor joist cavities and the insulation, if any. The subfloor must be in place to support the face wall of the dormer.

A shed dormer is built within the confines of a large rectangular hole cut into the roof. Essentially, this hole is the rough opening for the dormer. It's important to locate the rough opening on the sloping underside of the roof properly. First identify the rafters to be removed; then use dimensions taken from the cross-sectional drawing to snap two chalk lines on the attic floor. One line represents the outside of the face wall; the other represents the inside face of the upper header.

2 **Mark the Opening.** Use a plumb bob to determine the points at which the chalked layout lines "intersect" the two rafters (called trimmers) that form the outside of the rough opening. Draw a plumb layout line on the rafters at each intersection; then drive a nail clear through the roof where the layout meets the underside of the roof sheathing. The nails mark the corners of the opening.

Continued on next page.

Chalkline

1 Locate the position of the face wall and the upper header on the subfloor. Both are parallel with the eaves of the house.

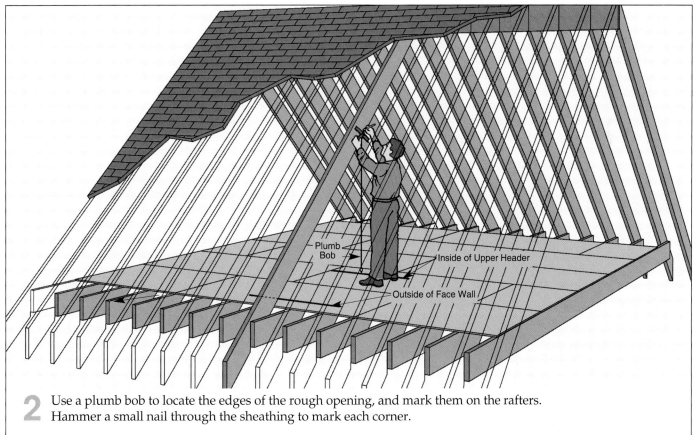

Plumb Bob

Inside of Upper Header

Outside of Face Wall

2 Use a plumb bob to locate the edges of the rough opening, and mark them on the rafters. Hammer a small nail through the sheathing to mark each corner.

Continued from previous page.

3 **Strip the Roof, and Remove the Sheathing.** Before you start, spread a tarp over the plants and ground below. Snap chalk lines between the protruding nails. Then pound each nail back through the roof to keep from tripping on them later. Remove all shingles and roofing paper between the lines. Use a pry bar or flat spade to pry up the shingles.

Set the circular saw to a depth that just cuts through the sheathing. Use a carbide-tipped saw blade designed for demolition work. From inside the attic, use a hammer and pry bar to remove the sheathing.

4 **Mark and Cut the Rafters.** Most of the remaining work can be done from inside the attic. At the top of the roof opening, mark each trimmer rafter with a second layout line 3 inches from the first—3 inches being the thickness of the header. At the bottom of the roof opening, draw additional layout lines, but make them 1½ inches

from the ones drawn in Step 2. Check all lines for plumb.

Use a crosscut handsaw or a reciprocating saw to cut one rafter at a time. Support the rafters with temporary braces before you begin cutting. Make your cuts at the second layout lines to make room for the header above and a "bearing plate," a kind of sill you'll install at the bottom of the opening.

5 **Install the Headers.** Cut three pieces of lumber that are the same dimension as the existing rafters to fit between the trimmer rafters. At the bottom of the opening, nail the bearing plate in place.

The two remaining pieces of lumber become the header at the top of the opening. Cut two shallow notches per rafter bay in the top edges of the header. The notches allow air to circulate from the dormer's soffit vents into the rafter bays above. Nail one piece of lumber in place; then nail through it into the cut ends of the rafters. Nail the second piece in

3 Set a circular saw to the sheathing thickness. Make the top cut first, and stand on the sheathing only while making this cut. Make subsequent cuts from the roof or the plank.

Temporary Brace Wall

4 Cut the rafters, and remove them one by one. If the opening is large, use a temporary framework made of 2x4s nailed into the floor and rafters to brace it.

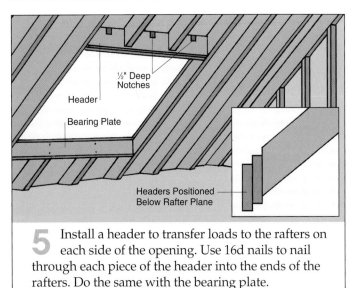

½" Deep Notches

Header

Bearing Plate

Headers Positioned Below Rafter Plane

5 Install a header to transfer loads to the rafters on each side of the opening. Use 16d nails to nail through each piece of the header into the ends of the rafters. Do the same with the bearing plate.

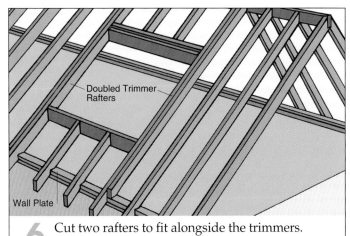

Doubled Trimmer Rafters

Wall Plate

6 Cut two rafters to fit alongside the trimmers. The tops of the new rafters abut the ridge; the bottoms rest on the wall plate.

place; then nail through it into the first piece. The two pieces will be offset slightly due to the roof's slope.

6 **Double the Trimmer Rafters.** Strengthen the trimmers by nailing another rafter directly to the outside of each trimmer. This "sister" rafter must be cut to fit exactly between the ridge and the wall plate. Use a sliding bevel to copy angles from the existing trimmers, and nail each sister securely to the trimmer rafter. Once the sisters are in place, nail the cut edges of the roof sheathing to the doubled rafters.

7 **Frame the Face Wall.** The face wall of the dormer is usually framed with 2x4 lumber, 16 inches on center. You may have to improvise the stud spacing somewhat due to the small size of the wall. Framing details for the face wall are the same as those for a regular exterior wall—be sure to account for the rough opening of the window. Cut one end of the corner posts to match the roof slope; then cut them to length to fit under cap plates. Nail the corner posts to the studs and cap plates, then through the sheathing into the rafters.

8 **Cut the Dormer Rafters.** You can get books filled with precalculated rafter tables for making cuts at various slopes. Beginners, however, find it easiest to draw a full-size rafter layout. Measure the appropriate dimensions for the header and face wall; then use a framing square and chalk line to draw a cross-sectional view of the header and face wall on the attic floor. Draw in the rafter, and use a sliding

bevel to copy the plumb cuts. The dormer's end rafters are doubled, and they get a different cut at the top because they land on main roof rafters instead of meeting the upper header. To find this cut, draw the roof slope line as shown in the drawing. Remember to allow for the sheathing thickness. Then lay out the pattern on rafter stock, and make your cuts. Hold the rafter in place to check for fit, and use it as a template for cutting the remaining rafters. Rafters must be 16 inches on center. The rafter-tail level cut must be at least 4 inches long to allow room for soffit vents.

Continued on next page.

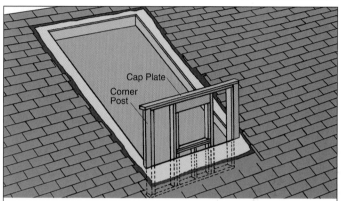

7 Assemble the face wall, and tip it into place. Plumb the wall, and nail it to the floor and the trimmer rafters with 16d nails. Toenail each stud to the bearing plate. Install the corner posts.

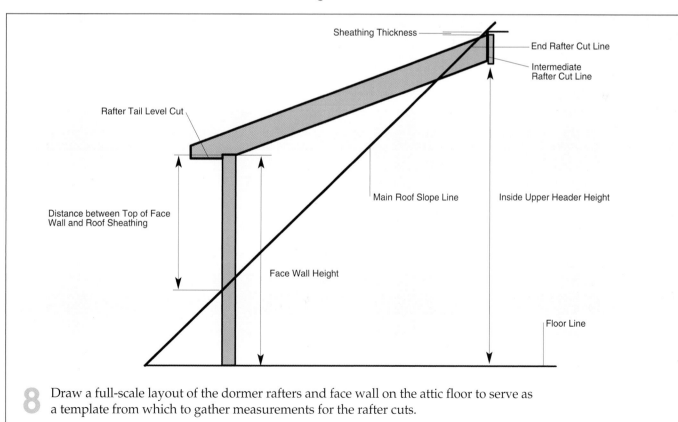

8 Draw a full-scale layout of the dormer rafters and face wall on the attic floor to serve as a template from which to gather measurements for the rafter cuts.

Continued from previous page.

9 **Frame the Roof and Side Walls.** Lay each rafter in place, and toenail it first to the header then to the top plate. Nail each wall plate through the roof sheathing and into the trimmer rafters; then lay out the locations of the sidewall studs. Cut the sidewall studs to approximate length; hold each one in place; mark the angle with a sliding bevel; and cut it to fit between the plate and rafter.

10 **Sheath the Dormer.** Use exterior-grade plywood or OSB for sheathing. Apply the wall sheathing first—it stiffens the dormer. Install roofing felt and shingles, starting from the lowest edge and working up. Where the dormer intersects the main roof, pry up the first course of shingles above the intersection, and slip the new shingles beneath them. Install the window following manufacturer's directions.

11 **Flash the Walls.** The metal flashing installed around dormer walls is much the same as that around a skylight. Install the base, or apron, flashing first; then slip step flashing beneath each course of roof shingles.

12 **Complete the Exterior.** Don't forget to install a rain gutter; water cascading onto the roof below quickly damages shingles. Route the downspout to another gutter.

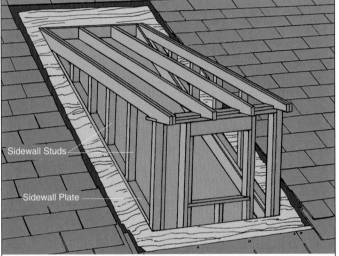

Sidewall Studs

Sidewall Plate

9 Use 6d common nails to nail sheathing every 6 in. at the edges and every 12 in. elsewhere. Use four roofing nails to install shingles over asphalt felt underlayment.

10 Nail a flanged window directly to the wall sheathing. An assistant inside the dormer helps plumb and level the window as you hold it in place from the outside.

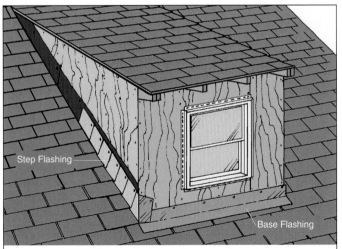

Step Flashing

Base Flashing

11 Install step flashing that matches the exposure of the roof shingles. Slip each piece into place as you replace shingles alongside the dormer. The siding laps the flashing.

12 Add and finish trim, gutters, and siding. Don't allow the gable-end wood trim to rest on the roofing at the top of the gable. Cut the trim short so water doesn't soak into the end grain.

Building a Gable Dormer

Most of the wall framing in a gable dormer is similar to that of a shed dormer, but the multiple roof planes of a gable dormer make it a more difficult project. Cutting and assembling the rafters sometimes seems complicated, but at least you've got the roof framing of your own house to serve as a model. The trickiest part of gable framing arises in places where the dormer meets the surrounding roof—at the valleys. The compound angles at the valleys makes this a project only for those who have advanced carpentry skills.

1 **Frame the Walls.** Install a subfloor; then locate, prepare, cut, and frame an opening in the roof as for a shed dormer. Use cross-sectional drawings to make sure you'll have adequate headroom. (See page 86.) You can frame the side and face walls just as you would a shed dormer or rest the face wall on a header as shown. The dormer ridge projects horizontally from the main roof, with rafters supporting it on each side. Note that the ceiling joists are in the same plane as that of the upper header.

2 **Determine the Roof Slope.** To cut the rafters to the proper angle and length, you'll have to determine the roof slope you want, which is the number of inches the roof rises per foot of run. The run is the distance from a

Gable dormers increase living space and add architectural interest to the roof line.

sidewall to the ridge line. In this example, the distance from the ridge to the building line is 4 feet and the height of the ridge at the top plate is 2 feet, so the rise is 6 inches per foot of run.

Continued on next page.

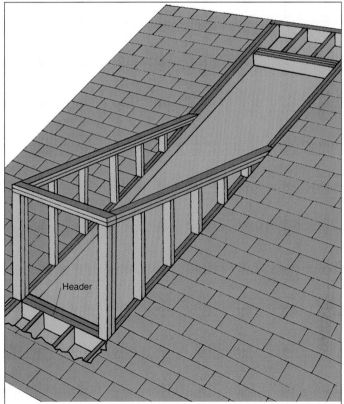

1 The walls of a gable dormer can be framed as in a shed dormer, or the face wall can rest on a header as shown here.

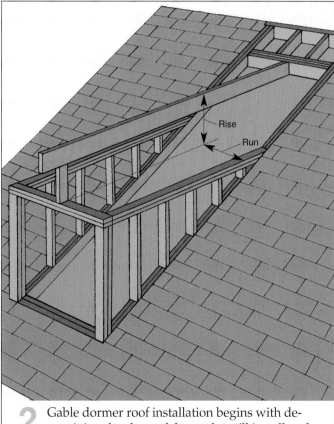

2 Gable dormer roof installation begins with determining the slope of the roof you'll install and attaching a ridgeboard parallel with the existing rafters at the correct height.

Continued from previous page.

3 **Set the Ridgeboard.** Center a 2x4 ridgeboard in the opening so that its top is 2 feet above the top plate. Cut the back end of the ridge to fit against the roof. Support the ridgeboard in front with a 2x4 set on end on the front top plate. If you've cut an odd number of house roof rafters, the ridgeboard will meet the center rafter at the header and should be nailed to it. If you've cut an even number of house roof rafters, attach the ridgeboard directly to the header. Level the ridgeboard carefully, and nail it with 8d nails. The smaller nails are acceptable because the ridgeboard only separates the rafters; it doesn't provide support to the roof of the dormer. Although this ridge isn't a load-bearing part of the structure, it must be correctly centered, as with the ridgeboard of the house, and leveled to ensure the correct installation of the rafters.

4 **Mark the Ridge Cut.** To create a cutting line, place the long arm of a framing square along the edge of a rafter board. The short arm, called the tongue, should be on the left, pointing away from you. Pivot the square until the 12-inch mark on the arm and the 6-inch mark on the tongue are aligned with the edge of the board. Draw a line from the top of the board to the bottom, along the tongue of the square. This will create a cutting line that will make the rafter fit against the ridgeboard.

5 **Lay Out the Rafters.** Mark the 12-inch point where the arm crosses the edge of the board. Slide the square along the edge until the 6-inch point on the tongue aligns with the mark. Repeat sequentially until you reach the building line. Place the 6-inch point on

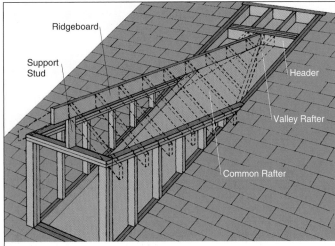

3 Attach the ridgeboard to the support stud in front and the header at the roof. Gable rafters run from the ridgeboard to the sides of the dormer and, at back, to the valley rafters.

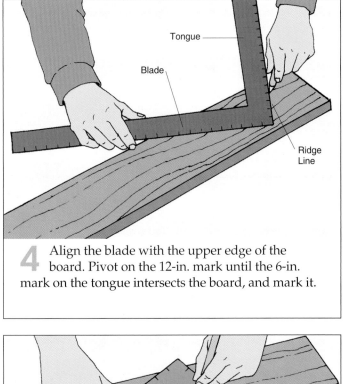

4 Align the blade with the upper edge of the board. Pivot on the 12-in. mark until the 6-in. mark on the tongue intersects the board, and mark it.

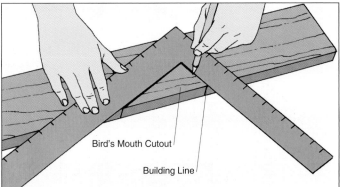

5 To determine the rafter length, lay the framing square along the ridge line with the rise per foot (6 in.) on the tongue and the unit of run (12 in.) on the blade, aligned with the edge. Mark the board where the blade intersects the edge of the board. Lift the square, and starting at your last mark, repeat for each foot in the run.

6 Mark the point where the rafter reaches the wall; align the inside of the tongue with the mark to draw the bird's mouth.

the tongue at the building line mark. Draw a line to the bottom of the board. Go back to the ridge cut line, measure back one-half the thickness of the ridgeboard, and draw a line through the mark.

6 **Lay Out the Bird's Mouth Cuts.** Now reverse the position of the square so that the tongue is on the right and points toward you. Align the inside of the tongue with the building line, and position the square as before, aligning the 6- and 12-inch marks on the board. Draw a line along the inside of the square along the arm and the tongue. This outline marks the "bird's mouth" you'll cut so the rafter can fit over the top plate. Now slide the framing square back toward the top edge, and align the 12-inch mark of the arm with the building line and the 6-inch mark of the tongue on the upper edge. Draw a line down the tongue to mark the end of a 1-foot overhang. Cut the rafters, and toe-nail them in place with 10d nails.

7 **Build the Overhang.** Notch the end rafters to accept 2x4 lookouts, or blocking, which will act as nailing for the flying rafter. Set the blocking in place; nail through the common rafter where the blocking butts it; and nail down through the blocking into the notched end rafter. When the blocking is installed, sheathe the roof with plywood.

8 **Finish the Gable Dormer.** The dormer is essentially a miniature version of a standard roof and is shingled the same way. Take particular care where the dormer roof intersects the main roof. Metal flashing beneath the shingles protects both valleys.

The gable dormer will have a gable-end overhang and a soffit on each side. Finish the overhang, soffits, and fascias as you would for a main roof.

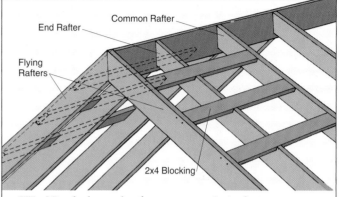

7 Notch the end rafter to accept 2x4s that serve as lookouts, or blocking, for the flying rafter. The rafter and blocking create an overhang and soffit to shade the window from direct summertime sunlight.

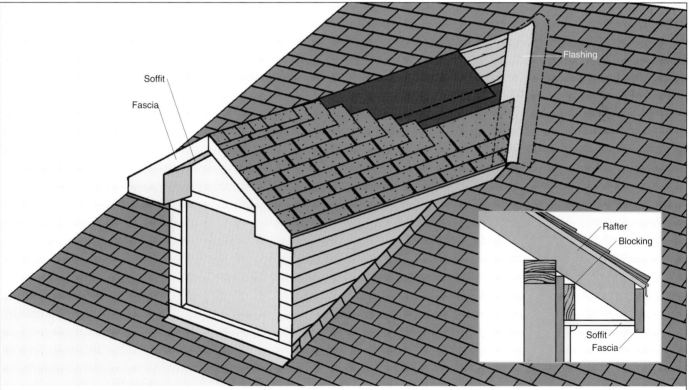

8 Build the soffits and fascias as you would for a main roof. Cover the plywood roof sheathing with 15-pound roofing felt, fitting it under the metal valley flashing. Start the shingles at the bottom, and work your way up to the ridge.

Skylights

The extra natural light flooding through a skylight can dramatically change the look of a room, which is one reason why adding a skylight is such a popular home-improvement project. Another reason is that it is fairly easy to do, although the job does involve cutting a hole in your roof. Skylights can be easily added to rooms of a one-story house or on the top floor of a multi-story house. It's a simple matter of mounting the skylight on the roof and building a short light shaft to the room. Where an attic has been converted to a living space, the job is even easier—you don't need the light shaft. (A skylight or two might also eliminate the need for dormers.)

Types of Skylights

As long as you are going to cut that hole in your roof, you might as well pay the extra money for what's called an operating skylight (the industry's way of saying it opens). The added fresh air, as well as the light, is welcome in most kitchens.

Aside from inexpensive all-plastic bubbles, most quality skylights have a glazed section attached by the manufacturer to a frame that raises the glazing several inches above the roof. There are two basic types of operating skylights: bubbles, which are hinged on the high side and open a few inches at the bottom, and roof windows, which are flat frames that pivot about halfway up the frame. In both cases the entire assembly, frame included, is installed in the roof. In addition to being cheaper, clear-bubble skylights expand and contract with changes in temperature. That motion stresses the site-built seam between the roof and the bubble, even if the installer sets the bubble on some type of frame added to the roof. For skylights with an integral frame, the manufacturer takes into account movement at the critical seam between glazing and frame.

Installation

No matter which type you use, the installation consists of attaching the frame of the skylight to the roof. Both fixed and operating frame-mounted skylights should install in approximately the same amount of time and require the same amount of maintenance.

Solar Tubes

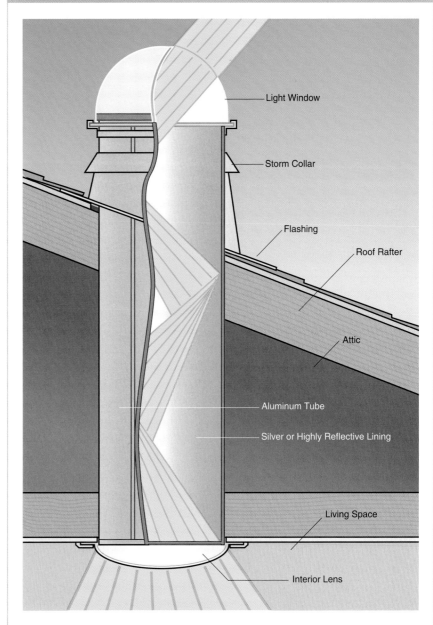

A solar tube, above, makes only a small opening in the roof and the ceiling, and reflects light down its shaft.

Solar tubes concentrate natural light that radiates into the room below through a diffuser, right.

Skylights in cathedral ceilings (above) offer direct exposure. The cross-sectional view of a roof and ceiling (right) shows how a light shaft can be angled on both ends to allow for maximum light entry.

Skylight windows (above) can be opened manually or electronically. Some models have fold-out sections (right), so you can stand outside the roof surface.

Installing Roof Windows and Skylights

Installing a roof window or skylight is possible for some do-it-yourselfers, but before deciding to go ahead, be sure you are up to the task.

You'll need to do some of the work inside a cramped attic and part of it crawling around on the roof. If you build a light shaft between the roof and ceiling, you're in for measuring and cutting framing and finishing materials that have tricky angles.

When you have selected your skylight or roof window, read and follow the manufacturer's instructions. Your first job will be to locate the window location on the ceiling.

Planning the Location

First, use a keyhole saw or a saber saw to cut out a piece of the ceiling drywall about 2 feet square, somewhere near the center of where you want the shaft opening to be. Standing on a stepladder and armed with a flashlight, look through the test hole, and inspect the roof and ceiling framing to determine the final location for the opening. Although where you want the sunlight to fall is an important factor, you should also locate the ceiling opening to minimize reworking the framing.

Most skylights and roof windows are designed to fit between two rafters (or three rafters with the middle one cut out). You will need to orient the ceiling opening the same as the roof opening, ideally with joists for its sides. You

Framing the Opening

A skylight requires that you build two new rough openings—one in the roof rafters and one in the ceiling joists—as well as a light shaft, which will run through the attic.

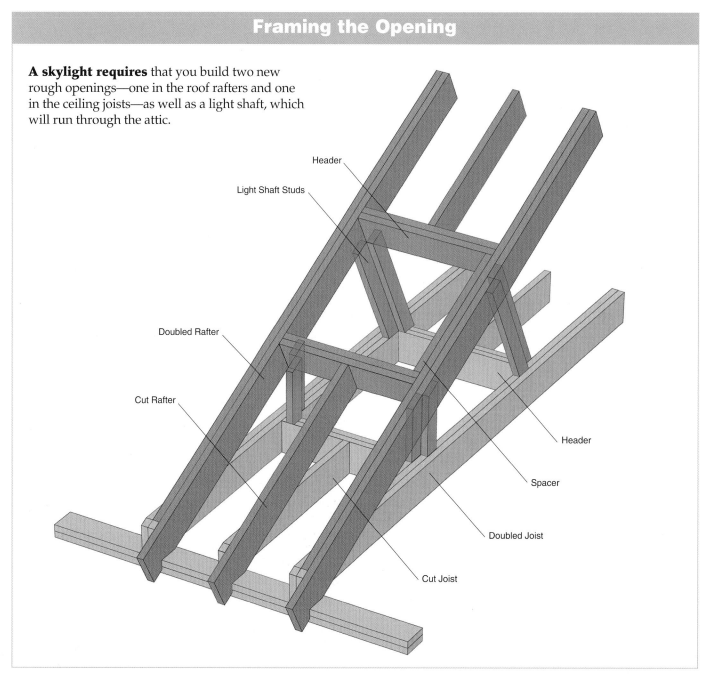

Header

Light Shaft Studs

Doubled Rafter

Cut Rafter

Header

Spacer

Doubled Joist

Cut Joist

can make the ceiling opening somewhat larger than the roof opening by adding a light shaft with angled walls. The end of the skylight opening nearest the eaves is usually directly underneath the skylight, and the end nearest the roof's ridge flares out to allow in more light. (See "Framing the Opening," opposite.)

Cutting the Ceiling Opening

When you have decided where the skylight will go, remove the insulation at that spot in the attic, and mark the final opening of the bottom of your light shaft on the ceiling drywall. Cut along the outline using a keyhole saw or reciprocating saw, and remove the ceiling drywall or plaster. If there is a joist in the middle of the opening, don't cut it until you're ready to frame the new opening. When you are ready, you will need to add headers to carry the weight of the missing joists.

Installing the Skylight

Begin by marking the location of the light shaft opening on the ceiling and driving a nail through the ceiling at each corner. Then go up into the attic; remove the insulation from above this area; and transfer the location of the four nails to the rafters above using a plumb line.

Reinforce the rafters by nailing 2x4 braces across them, above and below the opening. Then lay out the position of the headers at the bottom and top of the opening using a sliding T-bevel. Cut the hole in the roof as shown below, and install the window. Remember, all roof openings need to be flashed. Some skylights have integral flashing. But for many skylights and roof windows, this usually means weaving aluminum step flashing between each course of roofing shingles.

Lay out the position of the ceiling headers using a 2x4; then cut out any ceiling joists that are in the way and install the headers. Cut out the ceiling drywall; and then frame the light shaft opening. Begin with the 2x4s that form the ceiling; then fill in the sidewall studs. Cover this framing with drywall, and add insulation between all the framing members.

Controlling Energy Costs

The biggest factor in the energy performance of a skylight or a roof window is its orientation to the sun. Units placed on a southern roof will gain more heat than those installed on a north-facing roof. In cold climates, purchase windows with a low-E glazing. And units with U-values below 0.35 are considered extremely energy efficient. To combat overheating, make use of operable shades or blinds.

Cutting a Roof Opening

If you've left the nails that you drove in at the corners of the roof opening, that makes it easier to snap a chalk line on the shingles to mark the opening. Cut asphalt shingles along this line using a utility knife and straight-edge to bare the roof sheathing below. Drill a test hole to gauge the depth of your roof sheathing; you want to set your circular saw blade at that depth so that you don't damage the rafters underneath.

Use the circular saw to cut the opening through the roof sheathing. If you need to cut through wood shingles, place a board below the saw. By doing this, you can ease the saw forward without bumping into the bottoms of the shingles. When cutting through the roof sheathing, keep in mind that you will probably hit nails, so use a carbide-tipped blade.

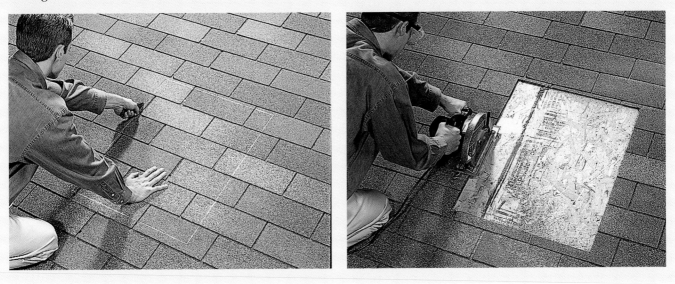

1. Lay out the light-shaft hole on the ceiling, and drive a nail through the drywall at each corner. Then transfer the location of these nails to the roof rafters using a plumb line. Connect these marks with heavy lines drawn on the sheathing.

2. Reinforce the rafters by nailing 2x4s across the rafters above and below the marked opening. Then establish the four corners of the opening by driving nails up from each corner so that they poke through the top surface of the roof.

3. Cut away the roof shingles and sheathing, as shown on page 97. Then mark the location of the support headers at the bottom and top of the opening.

4. Cut out any rafters that fall within the opening, and install headers above and below to carry the load of the missing rafters.

5. Install the window unit according to the manufacturer's instructions. Make sure that any mounting hardware is securely screwed to the roof.

6. The window has to be properly flashed to prevent leaks. Different manufacturers have different approaches. But usually step flashing is installed between every layer of shingles.

7. Use 2x4s to frame the light shaft. Hold a straight one between the two openings to mark the location of both headers that support any ceiling joists that were removed.

8. Cut and nail headers to both ends of the ceiling opening to carry the weight of the missing joists. Once the headers are installed, cut out the ceiling drywall and screw the drywall to the perimeter of the opening with drywall screws.

9. Build a frame around the opening using 2x4s. Install the angled members first, then the short studs. Once the framing is done, install drywall on the inside surface. Add insulation between the framing members on the attic side of the light shaft.

repairs

Tracing Roof Leaks

The best way to detect a leak is to locate dampness or a trail of discoloration in the attic. Do not, however, expect the leak to be directly above a damp ceiling or wall. Most likely the leaking water has traveled beneath the roofing material and down a rafter or truss member before appearing on the interior ceiling or wall.

The best way to find a leak is to examine the underside of the roof from the attic. If your attic does not have a floor, be careful to step only on the floor joists (never step on the insulation between the joists). Better yet, set boards or a piece of ½-inch plywood perpendicular to the joists. Make sure the ends of the lumber extend far enough past each joist to prevent tipping.

With a powerful light source, inspect the undersides of the sheathing in the general area where the stain has appeared. Sheathing is usually made up of plywood but yours may be made of shiplap planks. In the case of very old houses, you may find no roof sheathing, only lath nailed across the rafters with wooden or slate shingles nailed on top of the lath. Good sheathing or lath is uniformly aged and completely dry even after a rain. Check for dampness and discoloration and pay special attention to the places where the roof is penetrated by the chimney, air vent, or plumbing vent pipes. If sheathing is dark, damp, or crumbling, check for wood rot by probing with a screwdriver. Rotten wood must be replaced.

Water always runs in a downward direction so once you find dampness search for the source of the water's path above the moisture. Water may pool on flat surfaces, but it always finds its way downward, even if it runs along what appears to be a horizontal surface.

When the leak is discovered, mark the area to be repaired. If you are going to make the repair immediately, pierce through the sheathing from underneath with a nail, extended drill bit, or awl. If not, measure from the attic wall framing and ridge or eaves. Allow for the thickness of the wall and the outward extension of the eaves when taking measurements.

Making Emergency Roof Repairs

Damage from fallen tree limbs, violent storms, and exceptional snow buildup is an unwelcome surprise. Here are some interior and exterior solutions to leaks.

Limiting the Damage. Limit the water damage as quickly as possible by placing a bucket as close to the leak as possible. Remove and discard soaked attic insulation. A string attached to the leak guides the water to the bucket.

Providing Protection. Cover large areas of damage with a fiber-reinforced plastic dropcloth. Place boards under the dropcloth to create a high spot that will carry water away from the damaged area.

Fixing a Shingle. To fix a broken or missing shingle in an emergency situation, slip a piece of scrap sheet metal or aluminum flashing under the damaged shingle. Tap it with a block of wood to force it under the course above.

Limiting the Damage. Catch the water as soon as possible; mop up and remove any soaked materials.

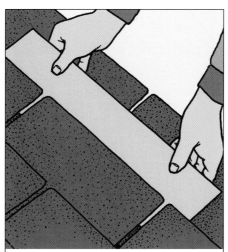

Fixing a Shingle. A simple piece of metal shoved under a shingle tab holds until a more permanent patch is made.

Providing Protection. Cover the leak if possible to prevent additional damage.

Locating Trouble Spots

If your roof has a leak check the trouble spots to determine where the leak originates. Trouble spots are those places well known for causing leaks. They include valleys, flashing along walls and around objects that penetrate the roof (such as chimneys, air vents, and plumbing stacks), rotting doors, gutters, eaves encrusted with ice, and popped nails. Keep in mind that almost all flat roofs eventually experience problems.

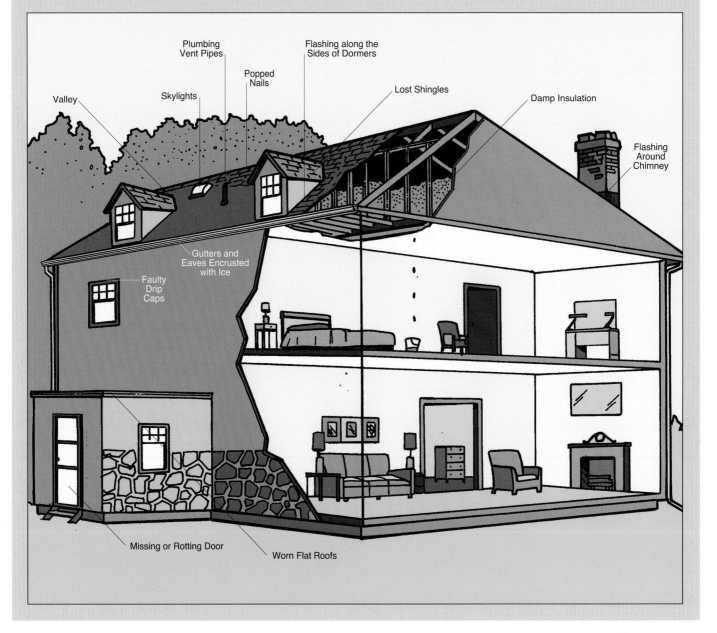

Making Temporary Roof Repairs

Equipped with a hammer, a pry bar, galvanized roofing nails, roofing cement, and spare shingles, a do-it-yourselfer can quickly make repairs to protect the home temporarily. When dealing with shingles remember to tuck the topmost edge of new shingles or patches beneath the course above. This overlap sheds water in a downward direction.

To temporarily repair wind-torn shingles, glue down both sides of the tear with roofing cement. Nail both sides and apply cement over the heads of the nails. Applying a small amount of cement to the shank of the nail before hammering it home creates an especially good seal. In a similar fashion, curled shingles are glued down with roofing cement. This is best done on a hot day when the shingles are warm and supple. Nail them if necessary, coating the nail shanks and heads with roofing cement.

Repairing Blisters on Built-Up Roofs

With time, blisters may appear on built-up roofs. This occurs because moisture that is trapped under one of the layers of the roof expands due to extreme heat and causes bubbles to form. The bubbles must be lanced, flattened, and resealed to eliminate the possibility of a future leak.

1 Splitting the Blister. Begin by lancing the blister with a utility knife. Take care not to damage the layers underneath. Allow moisture beneath the blister to dry.

2 Applying Roofing Cement. Before flattening, apply a generous layer of roofing cement into the blistered area. Be sure to work the cement well under the interior edges. Nail the patch in place.

3 Applying a Patch. Use a piece of 90-pound roofing paper to cut out a patch that is at least 3 inches larger than the blistered area in all directions. Nail down the patch, and cover the entire area with roofing cement.

4 Re-applying Gravel. If weather permits, let the patch dry for several days. Then pour roofing tar (not cement) onto the patch, and evenly sprinkle pea gravel over the patch so that it matches the rest of the roof.

1 Cut the blister open using a utility knife without damaging the layers underneath.

2 Push roofing cement under the edges of the blister.

3 Cut a patch larger than the damaged area, and nail every 2 in. around the perimeter. Cover with roofing cement.

4 After letting the patch dry, coat the area with roofing tar and cover it with pea gravel.

1. Remove Gravel. With a flat spade, scrape away surface gravel from the damaged area.

2. Cut damaged area. Cut away a rectangular piece around the damaged section using a utility knife.

3. Apply Roofing Cement. Fill up the removed patch area with a generous amount of roofing cement.

4. Apply Reinforcement. Strengthen the patch material by applying fiberglass mesh to the area.

5. Cover the Patch. Use a mason's trowel to cover the patched area with roofing cement.

6. Apply Gravel. Replace the gravel, called ballast, over the patched area. The gravel protects the surface.

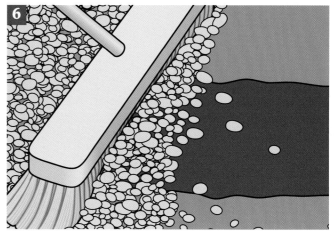

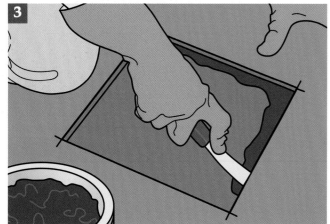

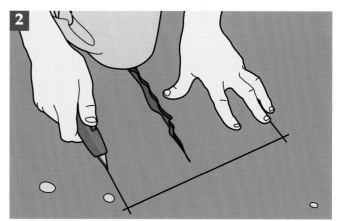

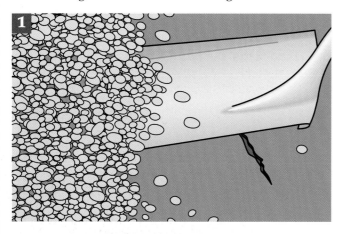

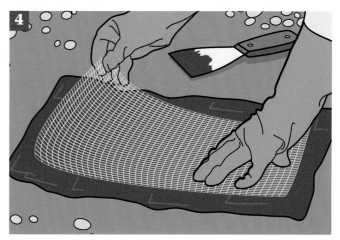

Making Permanent Shingle Repairs

If the roof is sound except for some isolated shingle damage, there is a way to repair composition shingles. To make your working area as safe and convenient as possible while making these repairs, note the information on ladders and roof brackets. (See page 10.)

1 Removing Nails. Each shingle is held in place by two sets of four nails: one set directly pierces the shingle and the other pierces the shingle after passing through the course above. Remove the damaged shingle by first pulling out the nails that pass through the shingle above into the damaged shingle. Then pull out the nails that pass directly through the damaged shingle. To get at the nails, hold the tabs back and use a flat pry bar to pry out the nails. You may need to release the adhesive seals by levering underneath with the pry bar, but be careful not to crack the shingle when working in cooler weather.

2 Replacing the Shingle. Slip a new shingle in place, aligning it with the tabs on either side. If the weather is warm enough to make the tabs supple, simply bend them up and nail the shingle in place with galvanized roofing nails.

If you are making the repair in cool weather, you may want to use the flat end of a crowbar or pry bar to hammer the nail. Hammer on the bar as near as possible to the nailhead without hitting the shingles.

3 Sealing the Shingle. Place a small amount of roofing cement under the tabs and press down. This holds shingles down until they settle into place with warm weather.

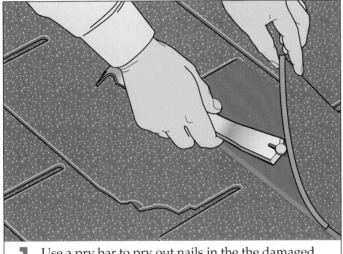

1 Use a pry bar to pry out nails in the the damaged shingle and in the course above.

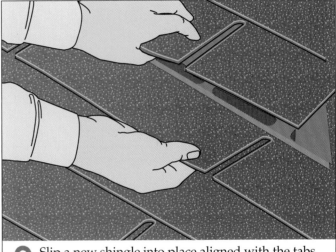

2 Slip a new shingle into place aligned with the tabs on either side.

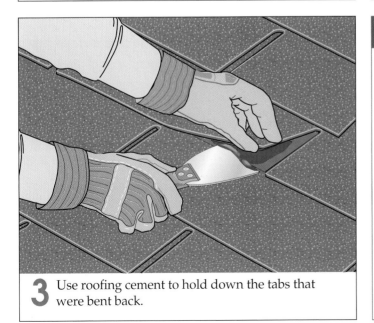

3 Use roofing cement to hold down the tabs that were bent back.

Repairing a Ridge Shingle

A crack in the ridge (usually caused by a fallen tree limb) is repaired by cutting a shingle tab to size and cementing it in place. Bend the patch gently to match the curve of the ridge, and slip one edge of it under the lip of the ridge shingle nearest the damage.

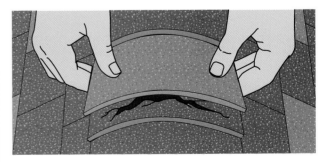

Repairing Wood Shingles and Shakes

1. Splitting and Removing the Shingle. Remove damaged shingles by splitting them using a sharp chisel and cutting out the damaged area.

2. Cutting Nails. Insert wedges to raise the overlapping shingle. Use a hacksaw blade (wrap electrical tape around one end to spare your fingers) to cut the nails that remain in the damaged shingle.

3. Trim the New Shingle. There should be a ⅛-inch gap on both sides of the replacement shingle.

4. Forcing the Shingle into Place. Push the shingle up to about 1 inch of the course line. Toenail it in place. Use a nail set to drive the nails below the surface (top). Use a wood block to drive the shingle home, which places the nailheads under the overlapping course (bottom).

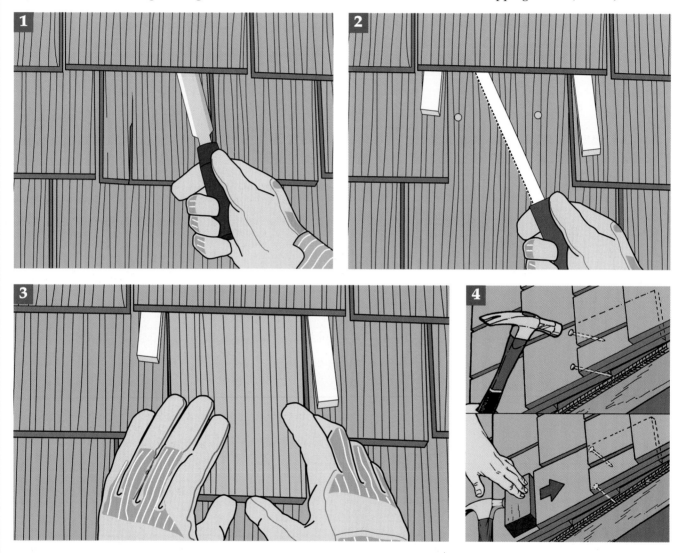

Repairing Cracks and Splits

You can patch minor cracks (up to ½ inch) using roofing cement. Simply spread the cement over the crack. For larger cracks, apply a couple of dabs of roofing cement to the underside of a piece of sheet aluminum, and slip it under the shingle. Fix bowed shingles or shakes by splitting the bowed shingles lengthwise with a chisel. Remove about ¼ inch of the shingle at the split so that it lies down flat. Drill pilot holes, and nail each side of the split. Finish the job by applying a coat of roofing cement over the split.

Repairing Fascia and Eaves Damage

1 **Removing the Gutter.** To rebuild a section of eaves, remove the overlapping run of gutter. Support both ends of the gutter while lowering it to the ground.

2 **Removing Damaged Wood.** Pry off the damaged fascia from the rafter ends. If a complete fascia board is not removed, make a cut over the middle of a rafter end. If the end of the rafter is too chewed up to provide good nailing, add a small nailing block to the side of the rafter flush to the end.

3 **Replacing Eaves Fascia.** Cut new boards to length, and prime on both sides. If you are working alone, hammer a nail into the top edge of the new fascia; then bend it over and use it as a hook to hold one end in place while you nail the other end.

4 **Straightening New Wood.** Hammer two 8d galvanized nails (one above the other) at each rafter. Stretch a string or chalk line to determine where the board bows or cups. Tap from behind in cupped sections; insert builder's shims where needed.

Flashing is the crucial water barrier between the roof and vertical surfaces such as chimneys, vents, and walls. Most roof leaks can be blamed on damaged flashing, such as bent or loose metal flashing, or worn or punctured roll roofing. Simply bend pieces of metal flashing to their original shape; then renail and caulk with asphalt. Flashing that is fitted into mortar joints on chimneys sometimes loosens. In this case, chip out the loose mortar and replace with mortar or latex mortar caulk.

5 **Replacing Damaged Soffit.** Remove the damaged area, including trim. Cut the replacement piece to size, and use the damaged piece as a guide to mark the locations of the rafters. Tack two 8d nails at each mark. (It is easier than trying to start the nails upside down.)

6 **Getting a Tight Fit.** Pry the soffit outward until you have a tight joint between the fascia and the soffit.

1 Pull back a shingle tab to reveal the nails holding the strap of the gutter hanger.

2 Pry off damaged fascia. To remove a section cut over a rafter, start from the saw cut.

3 To replace, bend a nail in the top of the fascia to hook one end while you nail the other end.

4 Set a taut line as a guide for straightening replacement fascia.

5 If it's damaged, remove the soffit. Start nails on the new piece before pushing it into place.

6 Pry the soffit outward for a tight, straight fit with the fascia. Replace soffit trim.

9 Repairs

Maintaining Gutters

Many old roofs have no trouble shedding water—as long as the water continues to flow off it. The trouble starts when water backs up in the gutters and drains. Leaves, twigs, and other debris can block drain outlets, clog gutters and downspouts, and stop up underground drains that take water away from the building.

There are many products designed to prevent blockages, such as wire baskets and gutter screens. In theory, wet leaves are supposed to pile up on them and then dry out and blow away, leaving a clear path for drainage. In reality, the screens and guards often clog themselves, particularly on flat and low-slope roofs. So instead of cleaning out the gutters, you have to clean off the gutter guards.

You may have seen advertisements for a supposedly clog-proof gutter, basically a strip of louvers. It simply breaks the flow into a series of small streams that drop off the edge of the roof, including down your neck while you're fumbling for the door key. They don't clog like a gutter because the louvers don't collect water like a gutter, but they dont take water away, either.

Blocked Downspouts

If water collects in a cleaned-out gutter instead of draining freely or you hear dripping in the downspout, some debris may have gotten hung up at one of the fittings. The most likely bottleneck is the S-shaped piece of pipe that carries water from gutters at the edge of the roof overhang and curves back toward the house wall to a downspout.

Most downspout systems have enough play that you can take them apart to get at a clog. Some are pressure-fitted together; some are joined with sheet-metal screws. Try flushing the debris out with a garden hose first. You may be able to clear the blockage without disassembly.

Gutter Hangers

Spikes and ferrules are the standard hanging system. The ferrule (a tube around the spike) prevents crimping.

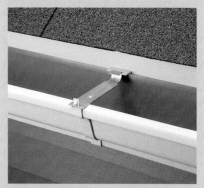

Brackets nail into the fascia board and clip into the gutter edge. Space brackets about 3 feet apart.

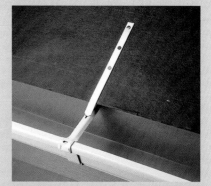

Straps wrap around the gutter and are nailed to the roof deck under the first course of shingles.

System Assembly

Metal and vinyl gutter hardware includes a full line of fittings. In addition to U-shaped gutters (and end caps), there are inside and outside corner pieces, connectors to link sections of gutters, drop outlets, downspout pipes, and a variety of brackets and hangers that hold the system to the house.

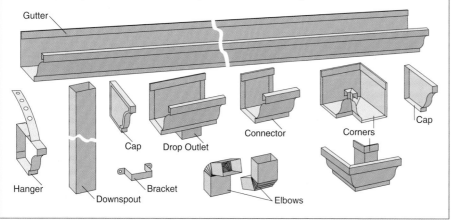

Gutter

Hanger · Cap · Downspout · Drop Outlet · Bracket · Connector · Elbows · Corners · Cap

Slope. Gutters should slope about 1 in. for every 10 lin. ft.—more for better drainage. Place downspouts every 35 ft.

Gutter Cleaners

Keeping gutters clean will help to prevent backups and leaks in bad weather. Clean gutters in the fall after all the leaves have fallen and in the spring. Start by pulling out all debris by hand; then flush the entire system with water from a garden hose.

A wire basket that rests in the gutter over the downspout opening will keep debris out of the pipe.

Screens that cover the entire gutter are designed to trap wet debris where it can dry and blow away.

Some systems replace standard gutters with louvers that disperse the flow onto the ground.

Downspout Extenders

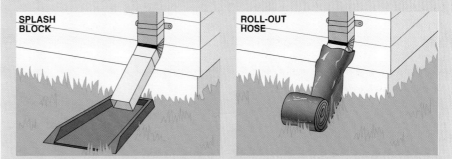

SPLASH BLOCK

ROLL-OUT HOSE

Splash blocks are designed to prevent water leaving the downspout from draining directly down along the foundation wall. Some innovative fixtures, such as a roll-out hose, extend to carry off water during heavy rains, then coil up again, out of the way.

Repairing Gutters

1. Use a wire brush around the hole to clean and scuff the metal. Cut a patch from the same metal as the gutter.

2. Set the patch piece in position, and drill pilot holes for pop rivets through the patch and the gutter.

3. Caulk the area covered by the patch and the back of the patch with silicone, and press the patch into place.

4. Secure the patch with pop rivets. Install as many as you need to make the caulk ooze out on all sides.

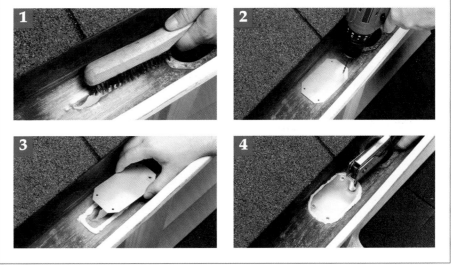

resource guide

This list of manufacturers and associations is meant to be a general guide to additional industry and product-related sources. It is not intended as a listing of products and manufacturers represented by the photographs in this book.

Amerimax Home Products
800-347-2586
www.amerimax.com
Manufactures and distributes metal and vinyl rain gutters, soffit and fascia products, and drip edges.

Asphalt Roofing Manufacturers Association
Public Information Department
750 National Press Building
529 14th St., NW
Washington, DC 20045
202-207-0917
www.asphaltroofing.org
Trade association representing most of North America's asphalt roofing manufacturing companies.

ATAS International
6612 Snowdrift Rd.
Allentown, PA 18106
800-468-1441
www.atas.com
Manufactures metal roofing and wall panels, roofing trim, and rainware.

Bradco Supply
34 Englehard Ave.
Avenel, NJ 07001
877-4BRADCO
www.bradcosupply.com
Distributes building materials.

Beacon Roofing Supply
1 Lakeland Park Dr.
Peabody, MA 01960
877-645-7663
www.beaconroofingsupply.com
Distributes residential and non-residential building products.

Brothers Roofing Supplies
105-14 Astoria Blvd.
E. Elmhurst, NY 11369
718-779-0280
www.brothersroofingsupply.com
Distributes roofing, siding, waterproofing, and sheet metal supplies.

CertainTeed
P.O. Box 860
Valley Forge, PA 19482
800-233-8990
www.certainteed.com/
Manufactures building materials, including roofing products.

DaVinci Roofscapes
1413 Osage Ave.
Kansas City, KS 66105
800-DaVinci (328-4624)
www.davinciroofscapes.com
Provides durable and authentic-looking synthetic slate and shake tile roofing.

Ecostar
42 Edgewood Dr.
Holland, NY 14080
800-211-7170
www.ecostar.carlisle.com
Manufactures sustainable, environmentally-friendly steep-slope roofing products.

Englert
1200 Amboy Ave.
Perth Amboy, NJ 08862
732-324-3900
www.englertinc.com
Manufactures a full line of formed residential metal roofing and aluminum gutters (including raw materials and accessories) mainly for independent installation contractors.

GAF
1361 Alps Rd.
Wayne, NJ 07470
973-628-3000
www.gaf.com
Manufactures residential and commercial roofing.

Karnak Corporation
330 Central Ave.
Clark, NJ 07066
800-526-4236
www.karnakcorp.com
Manufactures a full line of roofing cements and roof coatings for both steep-slope and low-slope roofing.

Metal Roofing Alliance
E. 4142 Hwy 302
Belfair, WA 98528
360-275-6164
www.metalroofing.com
A coalition of metal-roofing manufactures and related companies in the metal-roofing industry, the primary focus of which is to educate homeowners on the many benefits of metal roofing for residential applications.

Monier Tile
800-669-8453
monierlifetile.com
Produces concrete roof tile, including green roofing products.

National Roofing Contractors Association
10255 W. Higgins Rd.
Suite 600
Rosemont, IL 60018
847-299-9070
www.nrca.net
Trade organization providing information and services regarding replacing and maintaining roof systems to homeowners and commercial building owners.

Owens-Corning
1-800-438-7465
www.owenscorning.com
Manufactures building materials, including residential and commercial roofing products.

Quality Roofing Supply
530 Morgantown Rd.
Reading, PA 19611
610-375-8464
www.qualityroofingsupply.com
Distributes roofing and building products.

Rainhandler
2710 North Ave.
Bridgeport, CT 06604
800-942-3004
www.rainhandler.com
Produces an alternative to traditional gutters. The product breaks the water running off the roof into a spray so there are no gutters to clog nor leaves to remove.

Tamko
220 West 4th St.
P.O. Box 1404
Joplin, MO 64801
800-641-4691
www.tamko.com
Manufactures residential and commercial roofing products.

The Roofing and Supply Company
1409 Fort St.
Chattanooga, TN 37402
800-813-6189
www.theroofingandsupplyco.com
Distributes roofing materials, including architectural shingles, cedar shakes, and accessories.

glossary

Alignment notch A cutout projection or slit on the ends or sides of shingles that acts as a guide in application to secure a proper exposure.

Asphalt A bituminous compound, dark brown or black in color, used in the manufacture of asphalt roofing shingles.

Blind nailing Nails driven so that the heads are concealed.

Built-up roofing An outer covering of a comparatively flat roof, consisting of several layers of saturated and/or saturated-and-coated felt, each layer mopped with hot tar or asphalt as laid. The top layer is finished with a mineral or rock covering or with a special coating.

Butt That portion of a shingle exposed to the weather, also called the tab of the shingle.

Closed valley A valley in which the roofing material is laced or woven through the valley intersection.

Collars or vent sleeves Sheet-metal-flanged collars placed around vent pipes to seal the roofing around the vent pipe openings.

Counter flashing Strips of metal, roofing, or fabric inserted so as to shed water onto the base flashing.

Course Horizontal unit of shingles running the length of the roof.

Cricket A small peaked saddle built behind the chimney or over an entry. Its purpose is to divert water to either side.

Cutout Slot or notch in a shingle that makes tabs look like individual shingles.

Deck The structural skin of a roof over which roofing is applied. Most homes built within the last 40 years use plywood for this purpose. (See *Sheathing.*)

Double coverage A method of applying roof shingles that provides two complete layers of protection.

Drip course First course of shingles at the eaves.

Eaves Edge of roof that projects over the outside wall.

Exposure Portion of shingle exposed to the weather, measured from butt of one shingle to butt of next course.

Fascia Horizontal trim at eaves that covers the rafter ends.

Flashing Material used to prevent seepage of water around any intersection or projection in a roof, including vent pipes, chimneys, adjoining walls, dormers, and valleys.

Gable The triangular area of exterior wall of a building.

Hip The line of intersection of two sloping roof planes with walls that are not parallel with each other.

Hip roof A roof which rises from all four sides of a building.

Lacing or Weaving Interweaving of a course of shingles at an intersection of a roof; e.g., at 90-degree angles in a valley.

Laid to the weather (See *Exposure.*)

Lap To overlap the surface of one shingle or other type of roofing material with another; also the length of such an overlap.

Lean-to roof Has one slope only and is built against a higher wall.

Open valley Type of valley on a roof in which roofing material is trimmed and flashing is exposed.

Pitch Height from the joist to the ridge, divided by the span, or width of the building; expressed as a ratio of rise to span.

Ridge The horizontal line at which two roof planes meet when both roof planes slope down from that line.

Roll roofing Roofing laid from a roll of material.

Roofer's cement A quick-setting asphalt adhesive for use with roofing materials.

Run The horizontal distance from the eaves to a point directly under the ridge of a roof.

Rake A slope or inclination of a roof; the same as the slope.

Run wild To leave a piece of roofing or other material untrimmed until fastened.

Seal down An asphalt adhesive factory applied so that the shingles, once installed, have a concealed strip of sealing compound that securely bonds each shingle to provide wind resistance.

Sheathing The wooden foundation of a roof, also known as the deck. Typically made of ½-inch construction-grade plywood; older homes may have shiplap or planks.

Slope The degree of inclination of a roof plane in inches of rise per horizontal foot.

Soffit The finished underside of an eaves.

Soil stacks (See *Vent.*)

Span The horizontal measurement from eaves to eaves.

Square An area of exposed roofing 10 feet square or comprising 100 square feet.

Square butt shingles Strip shingles that usually have two or three tabs formed by cutouts or slots.

Standing seam The vertical ridge formed where two panels of metal roofing are joined.

Starter course The first course of shingles installed on a roof, starting at the lower edge of the eaves. It is covered by the first course.

Starter strip Mineral-surfaced roll roofing applied at eaves line before application of shingles. Fills spaces of cutouts and joints.

Stepped flashing Flashing along a roof slope against a wall or chimney. Usually consists of L-shaped units that fit into the joint between the roof and the wall.

Storm collar A flashing unit for prefabricated chimney pipe.

Valley The line of intersection of two roof slopes.

Vent An outlet for air (e.g., ridge vents on a roof).

Vent sleeves or Collars Sheet-metal-flanged collars placed around vent pipes to seal off the roofing around the vent pipe opening.

Weaving or Lacing Interweaving of a course of shingles where there is an intersection in a roof for drainage (e.g., valley).

index

Photo Credits

Illustrations by: Vincent Alessi, Clarke Barre, Chuck Chezosky, Jonathan Clark, Wayne Clark, Tony Davis, Cathy Dean, Mario Ferro, Craig Franklin, Ron Hildebrand, Ed Lipinski,Greg Maxson, Thomas Moore, James Randolph, Frank Rohrbach, Paul M. Schumm, SFI, Ray Skibinski, Cindie Wooley, Ian Worpole

page 1: courtesy of CertainTeed **page 3:** *top* courtesy of CertainTeed; *center* courtesy of Western Cedar Lumber Association; *bottom* Mark Lohman **page 5:** *top* courtesy of Certain-Teed; *bottom right* courtesy of ATAS International; *bottom left* courtesy of Accel Roofing Products **page 6:** *top left* courtesy of Monier-Lifetile LLC; *top right* courtesy of DaVinci Roofscapes; *bottom* courtesy of CertainTeed **page 8:** *all* Neal Barrett; (except circular saw) *bottom right* Gary David Gold/CH **page 9:** *left* courtesy of Werner Ladder Co. **page 10:** *left* Robert Anderson; *right* courtesy of Pro-Trim **page 12:** *left* courtesy of Cedar Shake & Shingle Bureau; *right* courtesy of Meeker Cedar **page 13:** *left* John Parsekian/CH; *right* courtesy of Vande Hey-Raleigh Architectural Roof Tile **page 14:** *top* courtesy of Rocky Mountain Log Homes; *bottom* courtesy of Vande Hey-Raleigh Architectural Roof Tile **page 15:** *top* Casey Jay Benson, courtesy of DaVinci Roofscapes; *bottom* Ray Rosewall, courtesy of DaVinci Roofscapes **page 16:** *top* courtesy of CertainTeed; *bottom right* Brian Vanden Brink; *bottom center* courtesy of

DaVinci Roofscapes; *bottom left* courtesy of CertainTeed **page 18:** *all* John Parsekian/CH **page 21:** *top left* & *bottom right* Dan Lane/CH; *top right, bottom left* & *bottom center* Brian C. Nieves/CH **page 22:** *left, left center* & *right center* John Parsekian/CH; *right* courtesy of C & J Metal Products **page 28:** *top* John Pars-ekian/CH **pages 30–31:** *all* courtesy of CertainTeed **page 35:** *all* Donna Chiarelli/CH **page 48:** *top left* courtesy of Meeker Cedar; *top right* courtesy of Western Cedar Lumber Association; *bottom* Mark Lohman **pages 58–59:** *all* John Parsekian/CH **page 60:** *top left* Simon McBride/Redcover.com; *top right* John Parsekian/CH; *bottom* Brian Vanden Brink **page 66:** *top left* & *bottom* Mark Lohman; *top right* courtesy of DaVinci Roofscapes **page 74:** *top both* Mark Lohman; *bottom right* courtesy of MonierLifetile, LLC; *bottom left* courtesy of ATAS International **page 82:** *top left* & *bottom* courtesy of CertainTeed; *top right* courtesy of EDCO **page 83:** Jessie Walker, design: Magnolia Restorations **page 89:** Phillip H. Ennis **page 92:** courtesy of Sunpipe **page 93:** *all* courtesy of Velux-America Inc. **page 95:** *both* Freeze Frame Studio/CH **pages 96–97:** *all* courtesy of Velux-America Inc. **page 98:** *top left* & *bottom* Mark Lohman; *top right* courtesy of DaVinci Roofscapes **page 106:** *all* John Parsekian/CH **page 107:** *top* & *center left* courtesy of Amerimax; *bottom left* courtesy of Rainhandler; *center* & *right all* John Parsekian/CH **page 109:** courtesy of CertainTeed

Metric Conversion

Length

1 inch	25.4 mm
1 foot	0.3048 m
1 yard	0.9144 m
1 mile	1.61 km

Area

1 square inch	645 mm²
1 square foot	0.0929 m²
1 square yard	0.8361 m²
1 acre	4046.86 m²
1 square mile	2.59 km²

Volume

1 cubic inch	16.3870 cm³
1 cubic foot	0.03 m³
1 cubic yard	0.77 m³

Common Lumber Equivalents

Sizes: Metric cross sections are so close to their U.S. sizes, as noted below, that for most purposes they may be considered equivalents.

Dimensional lumber	1 x 2	19 x 38 mm
	1 x 4	19 x 89 mm
	2 x 2	38 x 38 mm
	2 x 4	38 x 89 mm
	2 x 6	38 x 140 mm
	2 x 8	38 x 184 mm
	2 x 10	38 x 235 mm
	2 x 12	38 x 286 mm
Sheet sizes	4 x 8 ft.	1200 x 2400 mm
	4 x 10 ft.	1200 x 3000 mm
Sheet thicknesses	¼ in.	6 mm
	⅜ in.	9 mm
	½ in.	12 mm
	¾ in.	19 mm
Stud/joist spacing	16 in. o.c.	400 mm o.c.
	24 in. o.c.	600 mm o.c.

Capacity

1 fluid ounce	29.57 mL
1 pint	473.18 mL
1 quart	1.14 L
1 gallon	3.79 L

Weight

1 ounce	28.35g
1 pound	0.45kg

Temperature

Celsius = Fahrenheit – 32 x ⅝
Fahrenheit = Celsius x 1.8 + 32